FROM GLORY TO GLORY

SPIRIT AND SACRAMENT IN THE WRITINGS OF PAUL AND JOHN

FROM GLORY TO GLORY

SPIRIT AND SACRAMENT IN THE WRITINGS OF PAUL AND JOHN

Rea McDonnell, SSND

New City Press
Hyde Park, New York

I dedicate this book to my family, Sisters,
and friends with whom I experience
God's gift of abundant life.

Published in the United States by New City Press
202 Comforter Blvd., Hyde Park, NY 12538
www.newcitypress.com
©2011 New City Press

All excerpts from Scripture are the author's own translation.

Cover design by Durva Correia

Library of Congress Cataloging-in-Publication Data:

McDonnell, Rea.
  From glory to glory : Spirit and sacrament in the writings of Paul and John / Rea McDonnell.
    p. cm.
  Includes bibliographical references.
  ISBN 978-1-56548-368-2 (pbk. : alk. paper) 1. Spiritual life—Catholic Church.
2. Catholic Church—Prayers and devotions. 3. Bible. N.T. John—Devotional literature.
4. Bible. N.T.
Epistles of Paul—Devotional literature. I. Title.
  BX2350.3.M35 2011
  227.007—dc22   2010050662

Contents

Acknowledgements 7

Introduction 9
   Invitation 11
   Spirit and Sacrament: Ways that God Comes Close 11
   Jesus as the Primary Sacrament 12
   The Spirit in Our Lives 13
   Paul and John: Who Were They? 14
   Background to the Writings of Paul and John 15
   How to Use this Book 19

Part One
Paul and John: Unique Approaches to God

1. Paul: An Apostolic Spirituality 29

2. John: A Sacramental Spirituality 47

Part Two
Jesus as Sacrament of God and
Our Response to God's Sharing Glory

3. Jesus, Word of Life 63

4. Jesus, the Dying-Resurrected One 73

5. Jesus, the Disciple and Apostle of God 91
   Scriptural Message 91

6. Jesus, the Bread of Life ... 97

7. The Human Situation: Grace and Sin ... 105

Part Three
The Spirit of Christ and Our Response to God's Transforming Spirit

8. The Spirit: The Active Presence of Christ ... 125

9. The Church, Ourselves: Sacrament of Jesus and the Spirit ... 148

10. Ourselves as Church: Sacrament of Love and Union ... 161

Conclusion ... 181

Bibliography ... 183

Acknowledgements

My deepest thanks to all my teachers of the Fourth Gospel and of Paul, especially my students and directees; and to the one who taught me most about praying: Bob Doherty, SJ.

Thanks to my current "small group" with whom I can always share scripture, prayer, Spirit, sin, grace, myself: Rachel Callahan, CSC, Miriam Patrick Cummings, SSND, Cornie Hubbuch, CFX, Mary Irving, SSND, Barbara Mansfield, Brian McDermott, SJ, John Mulligan, Nadine Ostdick, SSND, Felicia Petruziello, CSJ, Sean Sammon, FMS, and Nancy Steckel. Thanks to Madonna Therese Ratlif, FSP, for her help with the manuscript and Katie Mindling, RSM, for her help with the computer.

Introduction

Mystery both fascinates and sometimes frightens us. How God comes close to us human beings need not be a terrifying experience if we become aware: that is, alert to find God in all things. Because mystery is that which is infinitely knowable, we are never finished exploring the depths of the mystery of God, never finished discovering God at work in everyone and everything. God's work is transforming us into the very image of Christ, as Paul writes,

> Where the Spirit of the Lord is, there is freedom ... we behold as in a mirror the glory of the Lord. What is more, we are being transformed into the same image, from glory to glory. Such is the influence of the Lord who is Spirit. (2 Cor 3: 17–18)

"From glory to glory ..."

In all my books, I suggest various responses we might make when God comes close to us through scripture, prayer, every relationship. God takes the initiative. Biblical characters then respond to God's coming close in a variety of ways. "But in these, our days," as we read in Hebrews (1: 1), God comes to us not in thunder and whirlwinds and fiery bushes, but in the person of Jesus, the sign and sacrament of God in our world. God pours out God's love, the Spirit of Christ, given to us so we would not feel abandoned in the world and would continually be transformed from glory to glory into the very image of Christ. As we pray during the Offertory during every Eucharistic celebration: "May we come to share in the divinity of Christ who humbled himself to share in our humanity."

This book is an invitation, in the company of Paul and John as our scriptural guides, to develop a contemplative attitude toward all of life, to develop a biblical, an incarnational and a sacramental spirituality. For those accustomed to thinking of "sacrament" as the seven Sacraments of the Catholic Church, or as Baptism and the Lord's Supper in other Christian denominations, God's initiative through sacrament is familiar. For many, it is the weekly communion with Christ that makes their daily life meaningful. In this book, I hope that John's Gospel will show that Jesus who is *the* sacrament of God permeates our daily life and can be found in the most ordinary, humdrum activities. I hope that Paul's letters will help you discover that the Spirit of Christ lives and breathes in every breath we take.

As the nineteenth century Jesuit poet Gerard Manley Hopkins expressed it: "The world is charged with the grandeur of God." And so is each one of us charged with the glory of God, glory poured out, glory shared. In looking at and listening contemplatively to all of life, we can discover Christ and his Spirit, and ourselves in relation to them. We can discover the sacramentality of all creation, its God-given glory, and ours.

For me, the ocean is a powerful sign of God's limitless depth of faithful love, a sacrament of the Spirit encircling the globe, feeding numberless people and buoying me up in play. So it was to the ocean in Rockport, Massachusetts that I traveled when I finished my scripture degree. I sat on the rocks and gratefully told God, "Now I am ready. I would be delighted to set people free by teaching." A voice boomed back to me, "Who sets people free?" I was disconcerted. "Why, you do, God," and I quickly revised my suggestion. *"I* will teach truth, and *you* can set people free." The voice returned in the crash of the waves: "Who teaches truth?" My much smaller voice replied, "You do, God."

Then, the entire verse from John's Gospel came to me: "If you make my word your home, you will be my disciples; you will know the truth and the truth will set you free" (Jn 8: 31–32). I was not about to make disciples; that is definitely God's work. So I asked, with much more humility, "What if I help people become comfortable in your word? Then you can make disciples, teach truth and set people free." And so it was agreed.

Invitation

"Experiencing scripture" implies a delving into, an immersion into the scriptural texts. In this book the texts we will experience are those of Paul and John's Gospel. However, although grounded in the writings of Paul and John, this is not primarily a book about them or their communities. It is not about the literary form of ancient letters nor about Paul's or John's theology. Naturally, we have to read, study, and pray with Paul and John in the context of their lives in the community of the church. This book is primarily an invitation for you to discover God's coming close, transforming you "from glory to glory," in a variety of ways as you read and pray with God's Word. Of course, God is already near, the very Presence who gives us life. Praying and experiencing scripture can deepen our awareness of this transforming presence.

Spirit and Sacrament: Ways that God Comes Close

God is free and creative, and comes very close to us, personally and in community, in hundreds of different ways every day of our life. God is eager to reveal — and certainly does reveal — all that God is and wants through the inexhaustible experiences recorded in scripture. Besides scripture, there are two other privileged ways to encounter God. One is through God's Spirit. The other is through the sacraments: the Sacrament of Jesus himself as the enfleshment of God, and the other sacraments.

In focusing this book on Spirit and sacrament, I could never limit God's freedom to come to each of us in many ways. And yet, in the incarnation, Jesus becomes Sacrament, God's glory poured out in flesh. God embraces the limits of being human in a particularly clear way. In sending the Spirit, God expresses the desire to remain near us, even within us, always. This, then, is a book about God, coming close to us *in Jesus* and *through the Spirit*.

Jesus as the Primary Sacrament

What do we mean when we say Jesus is Sacrament?

Traditionally, we speak of sacraments as signs of greater realities, of God's presence working powerfully in our lives. But the word sacrament is not found in the New Testament. What we do discover in scripture is that Jesus himself is the Sacrament of God. Jesus is the embodiment or enfleshment of God. Jesus gives us himself as the primary Sacrament. The humanity of Jesus is not only a sign of God's presence and action on our behalf, but the very embodiment of God.

"It is the Lord," the beloved disciple shouts to Peter when he recognizes the risen Christ on the lakeshore. "I am Jesus of Nazareth whom you are persecuting," is the self-revelation of Christ to Paul on the road to Damascus. Finding Christ on lakeshore and roadway, finding Christ in all things, leads us to understand that Jesus is the ultimate way to know and be united with God. Thus, Jesus is a sacrament of God's life and love with us, a sign of God's life and love poured into our hearts and into our communities. "No one comes to the Father except through me," Jesus proclaims (Jn 14: 6). As the sign of God, the symbol of God, the way to God, the access to God, the experience of God in the flesh, Jesus is the ultimate sacrament.

Ongoing revelation which we call tradition has led us to define, over the centuries, some peak experiences of God's life within, of Christ's saving action, of the Spirit's love among us. The risen Christ established a community through his gift of the Spirit, and he left us the Spirit in this community, the Church. Although the sacraments derive in some way from Jesus' ministry, he left it to his community, the Church, to determine their particular forms. Throughout the centuries the Spirit of the risen Christ continued to teach, form and transform. Baptism and the Lord's supper are surely found in the New Testament, and confirmation was included in the initiation of early Christians into the community. Then, in the second and third centuries, the Spirit guided the community to offer reconciliation for major sin, to anoint the sick and dying, to ordain priests, to recognize in marriage a sign of God's love for all people. By the thirteenth century, we were ready to name those peak experiences as our seven sacraments.

These seven signs, rather than "giving grace" as though grace were a thing, lead us to share more fully in God's own life. God's life, in abundance (Jn 10: 10) and poured out, we call grace. Thus, our seven sacraments all flow from *the* Sacrament, Jesus the Christ. Living deep within us, Christ is grace available continually, moment by moment.

The Spirit in Our Lives

As we examine and pray with passages from the letters of Paul and the gospel of John, we ask the Spirit to teach us, to uncover for us God's desire to give us all that God is. God longs to transform us from glory to glory, through the work of the Spirit and through the sacraments, which reveal God's faithful kindness. We will be pondering scripture in our hearts in order to foster our response to this incredible and irrevocable love of God for us. Through our contemplation of the Word, we hope to nourish deep within the actual experience of God's living and transforming presence. It is through the outpouring of the Spirit that we and every bit of creation are made one with each other and with our God.

Paul and John: Who Were They?

To help us understand more deeply and respond to our God who transforms us, we turn to Paul, a man who wrote, "Pray always, unceasingly" (1 Thes 5: 17). We hear in John's Gospel Jesus urging us to "... make the word of God your home" (Jn 8: 31).

Paul has been called the apostle of freedom. On the road to Damascus and many times after that, he experienced the risen Lord who set him free. God came close to Paul in Christ Jesus, in the power of the Spirit. And so, Paul becomes an important dialogue partner for us in our own search for a more free and a deeper relationship with Christ, in Christ. That relationship we call spirituality.

John has been called the apostle of love. Love was his experience of God through Jesus, and through the Spirit of Jesus poured out, both on Calvary and in the upper room at Pentecost. That relationship of love is union, the foundation of biblical and sacramental spirituality. Union is the goal of all prayer.

What was Paul's own prayer like? His relationship with God? Jesus? the Spirit? Can Paul help us "pray always," or has he simply overstated his case as he so often does? What was John's union with the Spirit like? Can John's Gospel open our eyes, ears, senses to the many ways in which God comes close, to the ways God reveals God's deepest self to us today?

We will not search Paul's and John's writings to find out why, how or when we should pray, relate with God, or even respond to God's faithful love. Scripture is not a rulebook, a manual of discipline, a primer for spiritual success. Instead, like the authors of scripture did, we will first question our own experience of how God has "always and everywhere" come close to us. Next, we will look to Paul's experience and then to John's experience. We will dialogue with these two faith-filled leaders about our relationship with God. We will try to see what in their relationship with God affirms our own experience, and what about their experience can stretch and challenge our relationship with our transforming God.

Hopefully, we will be able to see our experiences reflected in the writings of Paul and John, and yet live our life with God freely and uniquely. We do not want to use their teaching and experience as a measuring stick for our spiritual progress. Instead, we will follow the example of the early Church. We will live our lives in Christ and reflect on our contemporary experience of Jesus, sin, grace and reconciliation, the Spirit, the Church, and the gifts we have all received. Then we will turn to the teachings of Paul and John, which guided their communities in the first century, so that these teachings might illumine our own relationships with Jesus and with each other in our families, communities, and in our world today.

Background to the Writings of Paul and John

Before using the writings of Paul and John to discover God's transforming power, I want to set forth some basic presuppositions about Paul and his work, and about the author of the Fourth Gospel and his community.

Paul's Writings

There are questions in modem biblical scholarship as to which of the letters attributed to Paul are actually his own writings. Although all the letters can enrich our prayer, we will limit ourselves to seven letters which we are certain Paul wrote: 1 Thessalonians, Galatians, 1 and 2 Corinthians, Philippians, Philemon and Romans. Definitely not from Paul but from later Church leaders come the Pastoral Epistles: 1 and 2 Timothy, and Titus. Rich in poetry, Ephesians and Hebrews are inspiring for our prayer but were not penned by the historical figure Paul. Scholars are still undecided about 2 Thessalonians and Colossians.

This means that not everything attributed to Paul came from him. This is not duplicity in the scriptures, but rather the way the ancient cultures attributed letters to famous writers. For example, some think that Ephesians, which is not really in letter form, may have been a poetic summary of Paul's spirituality, written by a disciple of Paul's as an introduction to the first collection of Paul's actual letters. Another letter, Hebrews, is a homily that was finally included in the canon (the official 27 books) of the New Testament only in the fourth century when Paul's name was attached to it. And if this were not confusing enough, we also have two major sources for understanding the person and the teaching of Paul: Paul's authentic letters, and Luke's Acts of the Apostles. Scholars agree that Luke's writing is theological rather than historical. Unlike historians today who use microfilm and camcorders, ancient historians were not so interested in facts, verifiable data and details of events. Rather their primary concern as historians was the *meaning* of events.

Thus, in Acts of the Apostles, Luke can tell the story of Paul's conversion in three different ways. Or again, Luke describes the conflict between Paul and the church in Jerusalem in a more peaceful and symbolic way than Paul does in his own letter to the Galatians. In other words, we can get a feel for the early Church's appreciation of Paul by reading Acts, but for a more historically accurate account of Paul's work and teaching, we need to rely on his own letters. However, it is not history, facts and data which help us to pray with scripture. To read and pray with the Acts of the Apostles or Ephesians or one of Paul's actual letters is to deepen our love for God and our appreciation of Paul.

Paul can sometimes be misunderstood because we do not have all the letters he wrote to the communities he established. Nor do we have the letters which Paul's communities wrote to him, asking for guidance in specific problem situations. Paul may sometimes seem obscure or one-sided to us, because we have only a one-sided dialogue preserved for us, a side that is culturally conditioned as well. Readers who take exception to some teaching attributed to Paul might check on the authorship of those letters.

John's Writings

The history of the Fourth Gospel is equally complex. We believe that the Beloved Disciple mentioned in the Fourth Gospel is the authority behind its message. The author to whom we attribute a gospel may not have actually penned the parchment. But the author stands as the authoritative witness who originally handed on the faith. Like the material in all four gospels — the stories of healings, the sermons and parables, the accounts of the crucifixion and appearances of the risen Christ — the "bare bones" of the Fourth Gospel were shaped in a community whose members shared with each other their original experience of the historical Jesus and their ongoing experience of the risen Lord. All our gospels were first passed on orally. Only decades later were the narratives of Jesus' death and resurrection, and eventually parts of his life, written down. As the events were told and retold, each community remembered certain things and forgot others. When at last the gospels were written, they not only contained varied incidents from Jesus' human experience, but the varied colorings of the spirituality of each evangelist and his community.

For example, it would be obvious, were you to spend an hour reading Mark's fast-paced gospel before beginning this prayer-study of John's Gospel, how differently John and his community see the significance of Jesus and his work. Selecting very few "signs" in Jesus' public life, John's community reflects more deeply on the *meaning* of these transforming signs. (As we will see in chapter two, "signs" do not correspond to "miracles.") Over decades of prayer, contemplation and faith-sharing, the Johannine community is guided by the Spirit to penetrate the underlying reality of these signs.

As John's community let that reality nourish their life with God (their spirituality), they created long discourses in order to share their faith with future generations. For example, before Jesus calls Lazarus from the tomb, Jesus and Martha have a lengthy conversation about resurrection and life. This is the community's way of letting Jesus reveal the depth of this "sign." John did not, like a modem historian, take down the conversation in shorthand. These discourses attributed to Jesus are the fruit, coming many years later, of the Beloved Disciple's and his community's contemplation. They are an expression of their spirituality.

Having briefly examined how Paul and John wrote, and how their writings were preserved for future generations, we can now focus on the spirituality of Paul and John, and of the communities in which each lived and learned and evangelized. We distinguish Paul's spirituality as "apostolic" and John's as "sacramental." Paul and John both are so very Christ-centered that we attribute to both of them an *incarnational* spirituality. *(Carne* in Latin means "flesh," and thus our English word *incarnation,* the Word becoming flesh.) That is, we attribute to Paul and John a spirituality which shows us that Jesus puts flesh on the heart of God. Jesus gives God a body, em-bodies God's love and faithfulness. Both Paul and John staked their lives on their belief that, *in Jesus,* God has come very close to each person, to each community and to the world. In Jesus and through the Spirit, God is transforming all creation from glory to glory.

I invite you through this book not just to learn about the sacramental spirituality of John's Gospel but to experience it. I invite you not just to learn about the Spirit through Paul's letters but to experience the Spirit. And, by extension, to experience an incarnational spirituality as well.

Not only through personal prayer, but hopefully in a small group as well, your responses to God/Jesus/Spirit will vary. As in the first Christian communities, those varied responses will enrich you and lead to an open-hearted wonder and acceptance of self and of the other. When we share our faith, our experience of Jesus and his signs, the work of the Spirit in our personal lives and in our communities, the Spirit continues to teach us.

How to Use this Book

We begin by looking at the writings and communities of Paul and John, to see the ways God is portrayed by these early Christian writers. The format of this book is designed to help readers pray with scripture, focusing on seven letters of Paul and the Fourth Gospel. Its aim is not so much intellectual information as a hope for transformation through our direct engagement with the Word of God. In each chapter, scripture passages are followed by questions to guide your prayer and to suggest how you personally might respond to God's coming close. Because the Word of God was first active in the community settings of Israel and the young Christian Church, there are also suggestions for faith-sharing — whether with friend, spouse, family or small group — and exercises to help prayer groups or Bible study groups use these reflections together.

1. Questions

Each chapter opens with questions about your own experience, to ponder with the help of the Spirit who calls all things to our minds (Jn 14: 26). For example:

- What is your experience of Jesus — you, individually?
- How does (did) your family experience Jesus?
- What groups have fostered your experience of Jesus?
- What has been the experience of Jesus in your parish, diocese, country, worldwide denomination?

2. Scriptural Message

Then I offer brief commentary on Paul's or John's experience of how God comes close in various ways: in the Sacrament of Jesus and in the ongoing gift of his Spirit; in our personal and communal experience of salvation, mediated by the Spirit and the whole of creation; in the Church and the abundance of gifts poured into our lives by the first and greatest gift of God, the Spirit.

These comments merely introduce the central focus of this book which are the passages for prayer. We trust the Spirit to lead us to prayer as we ponder the meaning of the words of Paul and of the Fourth Gospel, the living words of God.

3. Guided Prayer Passages

Next are passages from Paul's letters and John's Gospel for you to read slowly, to ponder in your heart, and to pray with. These prayer passages are merely excerpts of their writings, meant only as brief tastes of the scripture's richness. The questions following the scripture passages are only examples of how to begin what I hope will be a lifelong journey of scriptural prayer. The questions may guide your prayer and may help you delve into the passage with more than just your mind.

I recommend that you read the scripture passage out loud and slowly, two or three times, savoring each word. Then, return to any word or phrase that tugs at your heart, that stirs some emotion or memory. If the passage seems to be foggy or dry, try one of the questions. But let the Spirit, not anything else, be your guide!

I also recommend that you use only one passage a day. Sometimes you might desire to return to the same scripture the following day. Because the Word is alive and active (Heb 4: 12), and because we are daily growing and deepening in wisdom and grace, the same passage may move us differently toward God even the very next day.

Once you have worked through this book with its selected passages from the writings of Paul and John, you may try another way of praying with these two guides. Slowly, read straight through one of their writings. Stop when the Spirit moves you to savor a sentence, to remember a similar experience in your own life, to speak or to listen to the risen Lord.

Introduction 21

A Word about Prayer

A working description of spirituality is simply being in relationship with God, a relationship which God initiates. Prayer is one way to express that relationship. It is our responding to God, bringing ourselves to God, Jesus or the Spirit just as we are: anytime, anywhere, in the midst of joy, pain, tenderness, anger, wonder, or sin. We can respond to God in quiet times and in sacred places but also in wordless rushes of emotion ... while waiting for a traffic light ... brushing our teeth ... when soothing a sick child ... in a gasp of gratitude ... in a question hurled at God ... in a flash of love for someone.

Prayer is basically the activity of the Spirit within us, calling out to God, crying out with "unutterable groanings" those desires which we cannot even put into words (Rom 8: 26). The Spirit is praying constantly within us, even when we sleep. Our conscious time for prayer, therefore, is like tuning in to the Spirit's prayer, just as tuning a radio will reveal to us some of the radio waves that constantly fill the air around us. The Spirit fills our hearts continually with the sound of prayer, crying God's name from deep within us and joining us with God (Rom 8: 15).

Because the Spirit is the one who prays, there is no such thing as a "bad" period of prayer. If we bring to God any emotion or desire whatever, even those labeled "unholy," we are praying. If we are angry with God, we are offering our real selves. If we are "distracted," we can trust that, since prayer is the Spirit's work, the so-called distraction may well be the Spirit's way of calling something to our attention in prayer. Even if we doze, the Spirit unites us constantly with God. (According to Thérèse of Lisieux, nodding off during prayer time can be an act of deep trust in God!) Prayer is not about our performance. Prayer is about God, God's initiating our relationship and deepening it day by day.

When we do set aside a special time for prayer, it is important to use as much of ourselves as we can to respond to God's first loving us. We can use our minds, wills and emotions when we pray, and also our memories, our imaginations, our voices in song, our bodies in gesture or dance. This type of whole-person prayer is modeled in the psalms. With the psalmists we clap our hands, dance for joy, make music on horn and drum, with compact discs or iPods. The more that our whole person is engaged in prayer, the more of ourselves can be offered and transformed by the Spirit into the Spirit's perfect prayer.

Please take a moment now to think about your past experiences of prayer. As you recall your own experience, ask the Spirit to help you reflect:

- How would you describe your personal prayer? Your family or community prayer? Your parish prayer?
- What was the prayer of your childhood like? Your teenage prayer?
- How did it change? What caused the change? Move in memory through the decades of your life. What changed your relationship with God? How do you feel about this change?
- What do you hope for in the future in your relationship with God?
- How much do you want it? How will you respond to God's desire for a deeper relationship with you?

4. Sharing Faith

After you take time with scripture for personal prayer, I hope you can find or create a group for weekly or monthly faith-sharing. In faith-sharing, each member of the group simply states what God has revealed during a time of personal scriptural prayer. Although you may choose to use these prayer passages only for your personal response to God's word, it is more consistent with a biblical spirituality to share the word in a group, because scripture itself was formed in small group sharing.

For example, the Fourth Gospel was the product of many years of faith-sharing in the community called John's. Members who knew the historical Jesus shared their experience of him. Others, who had never met Jesus in the flesh, would speak of their current experience in prayer of how the risen Lord, God's living Word-made-flesh, was teaching them, gracing them in the here-and-now of the first century.

Paul's writings, too, were formed by community faith-sharing. Paul did not write in an ivory tower, spinning theological doctrines. Rather, he wrote only in the context of a given community's needs and questions. He who had never met the historical Jesus deeply knew his risen Lord and was eager to invite his contemporaries, and ourselves, to know Jesus as he had, through religious experience.

In faith-sharing, there are no experts in Scripture, no right or wrong "answers," no sermons allowed. To share faith means that you speak only of your personal and unique response to God's initiating love. You dare to say in a small group:

- how and what the Spirit taught you;
- how you became more a disciple;
- how your heart was moved when you prayed.

This kind of sharing in a small community of friends prepares us to evangelize and express the good news in a personal way even to those whom we do not know well.

A faith-sharing group may simply be a married couple or family, a local religious community, a priests' support group, a Renew group or band of *cursillistas*. If you do not have a ready-made group, I encourage you to form a group of three to eight members who want to commit themselves to a regular meeting, preferably weekly, to share how God worked or what the Spirit taught them through their scriptural prayer. The group would need to set certain ground rules for itself. For example:

- a maximum amount of time for a meeting;
- an insistence on confidentiality;
- breaks for holidays;
- rotating leadership;
- whom to phone if unable to make a meeting;
- whether to serve refreshments, and other hospitality issues.

A Word about Faith-Sharing

While each group can set the needed "housekeeping" suggestions above, there is one necessary rule for faith-sharing, which brings to mind Jesus' own: "Judge not that you may not be judged." The rule insures that even secret mental judgments, not only of others but also of our own experiences of God, will eventually wither, die and no longer intrude in our faith-sharing groups. This rule, refined after my 35 years' experience of leading faith-sharing groups, is this: *No one may make any verbal response after each member has spoken.* To avoid verbal comments is a difficult discipline because so many of us want to assure others that we understand and appreciate their journey in prayer. However, even our reassurances and compliments are acts of judgment, though positive ones. And it is judgment — all judgment — which we must learn to overcome in the faith-sharing process. Sometimes our first judgment is, "Oh, I understand! I had an experience just like that." No, you did not. Everyone's relationship to God is unique and mysterious. In verbalizing that kind of comparison, you indicate that your mind was rushing back to your own previous experience rather than remaining open to receive the unique experience of the other. Sometimes judgments are comparisons of the other person's depth of prayer or beauty of expression with our own. While occasionally we might judge another's spiritual life as more immature than our own, usually it is our religious experience that tends to suffer by comparison. Even though our minds tell us that each person's journey with and to God is unique and that each person's experience is true, our culture is so competitive that we need to be counter-cultural. And so we make a commitment: in our faith-sharing, we will not compare, we will not compete, we will not judge.

The first step in countering interior judgments of our own or others' life with God is to keep from verbalizing them. Then gradually our private evaluation of others' prayer experiences will cease. Group members have testified that when they know that no one will say anything in response to their sharing, they grow more free and more confident. And those who listen experience a new openness to the multifaceted activity of the Spirit in each human heart. In over three decades of leading faith-sharing, I have noticed how deeply bonded such groups become.

Thus, gradually, the process of faith-sharing itself becomes a kind of contemplation. Contemplation can simply mean that we are open to and absorbed in God. In faith-sharing we are open to and absorbed in the Word of God as it comes to us through another's experience. To foster such an open and contemplative attitude in a group, I would suggest three simple steps:

1. Opening silence: Each time the group meets, open with a period of silence, three to five minutes in length.
2. Sharing: Each person speaks of his or her response to one or to a number of the passages from scripture which he or she prayed during the week. It is helpful to allow two to three minutes of silence (absolutely no comments) after each person's contribution.
3. Concluding rite: A leader/time-keeper needs to call for the conclusion of the meeting with some prayer or hymn or gesture such as a kiss of peace.

Suggestions for this concluding prayer are found at the end of each section in this book.

5. Small Group Exercises

Besides faith-sharing, other kinds of group activity can deepen the hold and the transforming effect which the Word has on you. Each chapter ends with suggestions for such activities and/or discussions. Using these exercises might also be a part of the faith sharing group's time together. If group members are not prepared for the small group activity beforehand, be sure to allow time for reflection before the group works with an exercise. Have paper and pens available for those who may want them.

Note that *discussion* differs from *faith-sharing*. In faith-sharing no verbal response is permitted. Discussion, on the other hand, is a free flow of ideas from all the members, but it is not argument. Often one comment triggers a further idea and then another, as the group builds what I call a "community truth," greater than what any member could think or imagine alone. Discussion without fear of judgment is another way people can experience the power of the bonding Spirit in the group.

Some groups have found it best to work once through the book, emphasizing faith-sharing on the guided prayer passages. Then the same group can work through the book a second time, now focusing on the small group exercises. Other groups have used the small group exercises at home in their families, keeping the contemplative atmosphere of their faith-sharing group a sacred time together as adults.

A Promise of Prayer

As you begin this exploration of how God transforms us from glory to glory, I will be praying for you and with you, that all of us may claim the transforming power which the risen Christ holds out to us, available to us through our baptism. Sometimes Paul calls it "the power of the resurrection" (Phil 3: 10). I pray that we might experience the Spirit: the prayer of the Spirit, the freedom of the Spirit, the love who is Spirit, God's glory, poured out and shared.

Part I

Paul and John:
Unique Approaches to God

Part 1

1

Paul: An Apostolic Spirituality

In the first part of this chapter, we will examine Paul's conversion, mission, ministry, need for co-workers and his passion in order to appreciate the depth and range of his spirituality. Paul's spirituality is as complex yet simple, as far-reaching yet contemplative as the man himself. Paul, a real person, relates with a real God-come-close in the person of Jesus. While acknowledging Paul's many ways of relating with God/Jesus/Spirit, we can most clearly characterize his spirituality as *apostolic:* that is, the spirituality of one who has been called and sent.

Paul is not usually ranked as one of the Twelve, but he considers himself an apostle because he was sent by the risen Christ to bring good news to the Gentiles. *(Apostolos* in Greek means "someone who is sent.") Therefore, Paul's apostolic spirituality takes on the characteristics of someone with a mission in life. This is important in fostering our own apostolic spirituality.

Like Paul, we can never be one of the Twelve. Yet if Paul is an apostle, then we too are called to be apostles. To understand how we ourselves might be considered apostles, let us see what happened to Paul to make him so certain that God had appointed him an apostle and had given him a mission.

Before focusing on Paul's spirituality, let us first reflect on our own experience of the man:

Questions

- What do you feel when you think of Paul?
- What do you admire about him? What angers you about him?

⁏ What teachings of his do you appreciate?
⁏ What statements do you wish he had never written?

Reflect, and perhaps jot down your answers. You may want to paint your feelings with water colors or magic markers. You might share your responses later in your small group.

Scriptural Message

After the resurrection of Jesus and the experience of his Spirit being poured out, the friends and disciples of Jesus began to proclaim the good news that the rejected, despised and crucified one was vindicated by God and now ruled as Lord of the universe. Heady news! Also threatening news, not only to high priests and procurators but to devout Jewish men and women who claimed God alone as Lord of the nations.

At first, the followers of Jesus announced simply that the one whom God raised from the dead was God's anointed, the Messiah. This was easily laughed off by unbelievers as ridiculous: a crucified Messiah! Then Stephen and his kind began to hint that Jesus was more, perhaps even the unique Son of God. Potentially, this kind of teaching could disturb the faithful, divide the Jewish community and weaken respect for the Torah, the Law of the Jews, which cursed anyone who hung on a tree (Deut 21: 23). According to this thinking, the truth was clear. Jesus, far from being the Son of God, must be cursed because he was hung on the tree of the cross.

A Pharisee named Saul was totally devoted to the truth revealed in the Jewish scriptures: according to Deuteronomy, Jesus was cursed by God. Not only was Saul learned in the law, but he was zealous with a burning hope that God's Word would find a home in his Jewish community. Saul energetically combated this new heretical sect of Jews and was commissioned by the elders in Jerusalem to stop the troublesome "Jesus movement" in Syria.

Paul: An Apostolic Spirituality

On fire with passionate love for God and his people, Saul hurried toward the city of Damascus.

Then he met Jesus, the risen Lord.

Conversion

In the Acts of the Apostles, Luke offers us three different accounts of what happened on that road to Damascus (9: 1–9; 22: 4–16; 26: 9–18). In addition, Paul himself offers three. In his letter to the Galatians (Gal 1: 15–17) Paul simply states that he received a direct revelation from God. In Philippians (Phil 3: 4–11) Paul explains his conversion as God wresting from him everything that he once counted so important. Finally, in 1 Corinthians (15: 8–9) Paul asserts that this revelation, this experience of Jesus as the risen Lord, changed Paul completely and gave him a mission, made him an apostle of Jesus the Christ.

How many apostles are there? Is Paul an apostle? Basically, an apostle is one who is sent. *(Missus* is Latin for "sent," the root of our word "mission.") According to Paul, the risen Lord himself sent him to preach the Gospel. As Paul will assert, argue, and defend again and again in his letters, Christ himself made Paul an apostle and gave him his mission.

The question naturally arises: But aren't there only twelve apostles? This is true, according to Luke. In writing Acts, Luke envisioned the twelve apostles as the heads of the twelve tribes of the new Israel, the Church. Thus, Luke thought it important to include a replacement for Judas (Acts 1: 15–26) so that the number twelve would remain. However, even Luke slipped and once named Barnabas and Paul as apostles (Acts 14: 14). And in the early communities, it seems that there were many more than twelve apostles, according to Paul. He writes that to experience Jesus as risen Lord is closely linked to being commissioned as an apostle (1 Cor 15: 8; Gal 1: 1, 12).

What consequences this holds for us! If we accept only Luke's understanding of apostleship, we are off the hook, so to speak, for we can obviously never be one of the Twelve. But if we affirm Paul's experience of apostleship, then each of us is a possible apostle. What happened to Paul on the road to Damascus can happen to us, perhaps suddenly or perhaps more gradually over time. We can directly experience the risen Christ. If we are willing, we can be weaned away from all that we once thought so important. We can be sent by Christ to bring good news. Like Paul on mission, we can journey to our own neighborhood, city or workplace to bring the good news of God's faithful and steady love to our often loveless culture. To experience the risen Lord as alive and active is to be called, like Paul, to be an apostle.

It is true that baptism has already made us apostles. But because so many of us were baptized as infants, it is possible that we have grown up Christian but with no felt experience that Jesus Christ is risen, alive and personally involved in our own living and loving. To know Christ as our Lord, our Savior, our Friend in a personal and vital way charges our life with new energy and zeal to share the good news of God's love made tangible in the Word made flesh.

In Paul's life this experience of the risen Christ is called his conversion. Saul was not converted from one religion to another. Nor was he converted from a life of disdain for God to a life of love for God, because as a Pharisee, Saul was completely devoted to God. Nor was it just a new intellectual conviction that Jesus of Nazareth was truly the Messiah. Rather, he was turned around *(con-vertere* in Latin) when he came to know, feel, intuit and experience that Jesus, who had been crucified and supposedly cursed by God, had not only been raised by God, but was meeting him, Saul, along the road.

From his own writings, we learn that Saul was converted from thinking he could "achieve" his own salvation by keeping the law. He was converted to utter trust that the dying and rising of Jesus was his only way of salvation. To be converted means to have a radical change of mind and heart. Saul's beliefs, judgments and values were all radically turned from his self-sufficient attempt to earn God's favor, to an attachment of his whole person to the person of Christ Jesus.

This attachment to Christ was nothing that Paul could produce on his own. Faith, seen in most of scripture as trust, an attachment of the heart, was God's free gift. The converted Paul found himself "in Christ." The indwelling was mutual: he in Christ, Christ in him. Some fifteen years after his initial experience, Paul could write, "It is no longer I who live but Christ lives in me" (Gal 2: 20).

Once, he had wanted to protect the Torah from the new sect of the Nazarenes, as the early Christians were first called. Now he was embodying Jesus and carrying on Jesus' own mission of bringing good news to the poor (Lk 4: 14–21). Once, Paul had been a scriptural fundamentalist, putting his trust in the "absolute truth" of Deuteronomy's curse. Now Paul was freed from rigidly clinging to one verse or one book of the scriptures and would cling to the living Word instead.

Mission

In the earliest days of the new community of believers, the gospel was offered only to Jews. Then, when persecution scattered the Christians' first preachers, they moved on to Samaria and Syria (Acts 8: 1–4), preaching the good news of God's unconditional love in Jesus to Jews and Gentiles alike.

An important aspect of Paul's mission was his preaching to the Gentiles. When Paul began his missionary journeys, the Acts of the Apostles notes that he usually went first to the Jewish quarter of a city. There, at a synagogue service, he would preach that Jesus was raised by God from the dead and was the awaited Messiah. If the Jews rejected that message (and they often did), Paul would turn to the Gentiles in the town and might find a more open response. But why, Paul wondered, should these Gentiles converted to Jesus be required to keep Jewish law, since God's love was available freely to them in the dying and rising of Jesus? God's love did not have to be earned. That love was poured out for everyone in Jesus, Paul was to write later, even while we were sinners, even God's enemies (Rom 5: 5–11).

Paul's willingness to welcome Gentiles into the Christian community without their pledge to keep the law was a problem for Jewish Christians. They saw themselves as a kind of renewal movement within Judaism. Their commitment to worship in the temple, to the law, to works of justice and charity, was increased by their experience of the risen Lord (Acts 2: 44–47). Jewish Christians saw themselves as the Nazarenes, simply another sect of Judaism, just as there were already Pharisees, Sadducees and Essenes.

For Jewish Christians, obeying the Torah might well have been a wholehearted response to God's love made visible in Jesus. But, Paul must have asked himself, was it a necessary response? Did the law unite or divide the followers of Christ? Could the law become a norm, as it had been in Paul's own life, with which to measure spiritual progress? And could this measuring weaken our call to trust? In his mission to the Gentiles, Paul had to work out these questions, questions to which we will return throughout this book.

Ministry

As we have seen, mission is our being sent to the world with good news. It flows from our experiencing Jesus as our risen Leader. In like manner, ministry also flows from our knowing Jesus, from our baptism, from our experience of the Spirit. However, ministry refers to our service within the community. Paul was not only missioned to the Gentiles, but he ministered to the young communities which he formed.

In the various cities which Paul visited, Jews and Gentiles accepted Jesus as their Savior. Paul would then nourish these new communities with further teachings, often staying with them as he earned his living making tents. He himself seldom baptized (1 Cor 1: 14–16). Nor do we have any record of his presiding at Eucharist (Acts 20: 7–12 and 27: 35 are obscure). Paul, not born into a priestly family, was not a priest. Rather, it seems that Paul studied the Jewish scriptures in preparation for his preaching. In Jewish tradition to study scripture is an act of worship and therefore ministry. From his praying with scripture, Paul would learn even more deeply what the dying and rising of Jesus meant, and how this mystery affected the life of the young Church. Many times in his letters, Paul continued this ministry of interpreting the Jewish scriptures so as to cast light upon current situations.

In his letters, Paul usually first proclaims God's goodness and grace in Christ Jesus. Then Paul exhorts, telling the community how it might respond to such abundant love. One of his common instructions is to remember the poor in Jerusalem, who were afflicted by famine. Apparently, part of Paul's ministry was to collect alms, thus linking different parts of the Church around the Mediterranean world. After Paul left a young community, his ministry to them would continue through prayers of intercession and thanksgiving, and on-going guidance through letters and personally appointed messengers.

Co-workers

Paul sent many messengers to the communities which he had founded. Because he wrote such authoritative letters we might forget how dependent this apostle was on his co-workers, both men and women. Barnabas was his chief colleague for many years in the mission field, according to the Acts of the Apostles. Paul's own major reference to Barnabas is sad, one of bitter disappointment that Barnabas could not maintain freedom in Christ when confronted by Jewish Christians about dietary laws (Gal 2: 13). Eventually these two apostles separated, and according to Acts, Silas then traveled as Paul's colleague.

Particularly in the greetings and conclusions of his letters we can see how extensive and dear is the network of Paul's co-ministers. Uniquely, many of Paul's colleagues in ministry were women, who played an important role in the communities founded by Paul. According to Acts of the Apostles, a businesswoman named Lydia led the household church at Philippi (Acts 16: 13–15). A tent-making friend of Paul's, Priscilla, taught the brilliant young scholar Apollos (Acts 18: 1–3; 26). In Romans 16: 3–4, Priscilla is commended not only as a co-worker but also for having risked her life for Paul. The message of Chloe and her people to Paul is taken very seriously and seems to have provoked Paul's first letter to Corinth (1 Cor 1: 11). All women in the Pauline churches must have prayed in public and ministered through prophecy as the Spirit moved them (1 Cor 11: 5).

A leading figure in the young church of Greece was Phoebe, a deaconess and co-worker of Paul's. She acted as an overseer or governor at the church of Cenchreae near Corinth. Called *prostatis,* which is mistakenly translated "helper" but which means instead a supervisor or governor (Rom 16: 1–2), Phoebe may have traveled alone to Rome to deliver Paul's letter to that community. She may have taken Paul's recommendation in 1 Corinthians 7: 34 to remain single in order to further the mission of evangelization.

Passion

So far, we have seen three aspects of Paul's apostolic spirituality: a call to mission, being equipped with gifts for various ministries, and his need for co-workers and community. Yet another aspect of an apostolic spirituality, Paul's and our own, is passion. Passion means suffering, and for Paul, it means co-suffering with Christ. Paul wanted *koinonia,* fellowship, union with the sufferings of Christ (Phil 3: 10). It may be that the passion of Paul, his suffering and prayer on behalf of his communities, affected the life of the young churches even more deeply than his teaching and travels.

The idea of co-suffering with Christ presents a problem. On the one hand, we say the risen Christ suffers no more. On the other hand, Paul's disciples teach us that we fill up what is wanting in the suffering, the passion of Christ (Col 1: 24). How can we understand this apparent contradiction?

In Luke's account of Paul's conversion, Jesus still suffers when one of the least is persecuted: "Saul, Saul, why are you persecuting me?" (Acts 9: 4). Saul must then have known profoundly how "if one suffers, all suffer" (1 Cor 12: 26). The body of Christ, his Church, which is being built up and is coming to maturity, also continues to be crucified. "We bear in our bodies the dying of Jesus," Paul writes (2 Cor 4: 10).

Sometimes Paul was called on to "crucify flesh with its passions and desires" (Gal 5: 24), not in order to achieve self-control but in service of the mission. He faced physical pain: hunger, cold, whippings, imprisonments, shipwreck. He endured mental pain: his concern for all the churches, his confrontation with Peter, his alienation from Barnabas, his humiliation by the Corinthian community, his frequent rejection by his own Jewish community when he preached in their synagogues. He knew spiritual pain, which he experienced in his conversion from self-righteousness and his continual hunger for God.

Through his suffering, Paul came to know God's own consolation. Paul also realized that what he suffered interiorly or exteriorly formed an ever-deepening compassion in him. "Who is weak and I am not weak?" (2 Cor 11: 29). Compassion means, literally, "to suffer with," to bear another's burdens. Paul understood that his co-suffering with Christ meant compassion with Christ's body, the community. In whatever we may suffer, we too can experience *koinonia,* community and communion with Christ and his Church.

Passion has two other common meanings. One is zeal, a single-minded desire and drive. Paul's zeal for Christ and his gospel seems admirable to most of us. Yet, another meaning of passion we find in Paul's life might distance us from this apostle. Many Christians actively dislike Paul because he seems angry, self-pitying, and arrogant. Paul had that passion which means strong emotion; he was a passionate man.

Jewish spirituality, as evidenced in the psalms and prophets, encouraged both feeling and expressing a wide range and depth of human emotion. Paul was undoubtedly an emotional man before he met Christ. After his conversion he let Christ direct his passionate energy toward preaching the gospel and toward loving forcefully. When Paul loves passionately, he can be tender and cajoling, like a nurse cherishing a baby. He can also be furious that God's faithful love is scorned, that Jesus' dying-rising love is ignored, that the Spirit's gifts are used for self-aggrandizement and boasting. He can feel hurt and angry when his own love and care are forgotten, misunderstood, even mocked. Sometimes his anger leads him to sarcastic, biting remarks, not only to or about his enemies, but even to his communities. Paul was the first to admit his weakness and sinfulness. His conversion was not once-for-all, but on-going. He knew he always needed saving.

Our accusation of Paul as proud and arrogant may not so much stem from Paul's sinfulness, however, as from our own misperception of how rabbis taught in the first century. When a Jewish rabbi gathered a community of disciples, he would teach them the Torah and its interpretation. He would also expect his students to imitate not only his words and values but even his mannerisms. Disciples walked, ate, talked and laughed like their rabbi. Greek philosophers trained their disciples in much the same way.

And Paul had been a rabbi. Thus he urges his young communities: "Imitate me." In other words, if you want to live the way of Christ, I will be your teacher. Imitate me: my teachings, values, zeal, compassion. Although often implicitly, that is what parents ask their children to do. Paul was both father and teacher to his new churches. Neither he nor they would have thought Paul arrogant.

In view of this, perhaps we could let Paul revamp our idea of sainthood. We have a two-thousand-year history of saints' lives, and their stories are often "cleaned up" by their biographers. Even Luke is somewhat guilty of painting rosy portraits of Peter and Paul in Acts of the Apostles. Paul's letters, however, give us a picture of an honest struggle for holiness. He writes passionately because he loves passionately and that means both with great tenderness and with great fury.

Paul is authentic in his letters, a man who needs God's saving love constantly because he has learned that he cannot achieve holiness, cannot earn love, cannot merit grace. Instead, he is saved through faith. Faith for Paul means clinging to Jesus, another man of great passion and now his risen Lord.

Guided Prayer Passages

From Galatians 1

> From Paul, an apostle not by human commission but by a mission from Jesus Christ and from God who raised him from the dead....
>
> Am I seeking the approval of human beings? Or am I trying to please God? If I were trying to win human approval I would not be the servant of Christ. I want you to know, brothers and sisters, that the gospel I preach is not according to humans. For I was not taught the gospel by any human being but I received a revelation through Jesus Christ. You heard about my previous conduct in Judaism, how fanatically I persecuted the church in order to destroy it. I had progressed in the Jewish religion far beyond my contemporaries, so completely zealous was I for the traditions of my ancestors. But when the One who set me apart from my mother's womb and called me through grace in order to reveal God's Son in me, this was so that I might preach Christ among the Gentiles.
>
> I did not at once discuss this with flesh and blood, going up to Jerusalem to confer with those who were apostles before me. I went away to Arabia, and again returned to Damascus. Finally, after three years, I went up to Jerusalem to visit Cephas [Peter] and remained with him for fifteen days. I didn't see the other apostles except James, the brother of the Lord.... Next I went to the regions of Syria and Cilicia. My face was

not known in the churches of Judea. They had only heard: "The one who had been persecuting us is now preaching the faith he was once destroying." And they glorified God in me.

God set Paul apart from birth to proclaim the Gospel to the Gentiles. Reflect on God's choosing you "from your mother's womb." When, where, how has God's choosing you continued throughout your life? Perhaps you could make a time line of your own salvation history, marking the major moments of conversion and grace. Ask the Spirit to show you where God/Jesus/ Spirit has been present throughout your life. Listen to the answer. Tell the Spirit how you feel about this choice and this presence, not only in major experiences but in the daily touches of God's grace.

1 Corinthians 15: 3-11

I handed on to you the primary things which I myself received: that Christ died for our sins according to the scriptures; that he was buried; that he has been raised on the third day according to the scriptures; that he was seen by Cephas, then by the Twelve. Afterward he was seen by more than five hundred of the community at one time, the majority of whom are still alive, although some have fallen asleep. After that he was seen by James, then by all the apostles. Lastly, he appeared even to me, as unformed as I was, like an aborted fetus. I am the least of the apostles, in no way worthy to be called an apostle because I persecuted the Church of God. But by the grace of God I am what I am, and God's grace has not been fruitless in me.

When Christ "appeared" to these women and men of Paul's day, they were called to be apostles, sent to bring to others the good news of Jesus' victory over sin and death. The risen Lord still "appears" to us and missions us to use all our gifts for proclaiming good news to the world. Being aware of the Lord's "appearance" to you means to have a very real experience of Christ, to know in your gut that Jesus Christ is risen, alive, at work in your life. Christ can reach the world through your life, just as happened through these first apostles. If that is your experience, thank him for being so real, so alive in your life. If you are not sure how alive he is to you, ask for an encounter as real as Paul's experience on the way to Damascus. Ask to know in your whole self that Jesus is not dead and gone but is alive and active in his body, in you. Now, listen.

Philippians 3: 3–14

> ... we who worship God in spirit and glory in Christ Jesus put no confidence in the flesh. I have good reason to put confidence in the things of the flesh. If anyone thinks he has credentials "in the flesh," I have more. Here are my accomplishments according to the flesh: I was circumcised on the eighth day, of the race of Israel, of the tribe of Benjamin, a Hebrew born of Hebrews. According to the law, I was a Pharisee; according to my zeal for the law, I persecuted the Church; according to the keeping of the law, I was perfect.
>
> But these deeds which once for me were great gain I now count as total loss because of Christ Jesus. I value all things as loss because of the excellence of knowing Christ Jesus, my Lord. On account of him I consider everything so much manure in order that I might gain Christ and be found in him.
>
> I have no more righteousness because I keep the law. It is because of faith in Christ. The righteousness that comes from God is due to faith in Christ. Oh, that I might know Christ and the power of his resurrection and, — if I am able — to share his sufferings, being like him in his death so that I might be raised from the dead too. Not that I have already received this, not that I have been made perfect. Rather, I press forward, reaching to grasp hold of Christ who has already grasped hold of me.... I stretch forward to what lies ahead ... the call of God in Christ Jesus.

Much had to be emptied from Paul's life. Before he was converted to Christ, he had clung to the law, to his own righteousness. He thought he was holy. That "saving" of himself through his good works was just garbage, or manure as he called it (Phil 3: 8–9). Now he wants only to cling to Jesus, even if that means sharing his sufferings. For us, that suffering will sometimes mean always running forward, never thinking we have finished growing, never congratulating ourselves that we have "arrived" in the spiritual life. Ask Jesus to strip you of your own ideas of holiness, so that your only holiness and freedom may be Jesus himself. Ask that he may live in your joys and loves each day and that he continue his saving death as you "die" through your small day-to-day sufferings. Pray that you may continually know the power of his resurrection.

Philippians 3: 3–14 (above)

Return today to the previous passage. Let it speak to you freshly. If nothing new moves your heart, work with these questions:

- Have you lost anything? Do you count anything as garbage because of knowing Christ? Tell Jesus how you feel about it.
- Toward what goals do you press forward? Be honest and tell him what you really want, even if those wants sound insignificant and maybe "unholy."
- How does Jesus feel about your goals? Ask him. Talk them over with him.

Philippians 3: 3–14 (above)

A third time return to this important piece of Paul's autobiography. First, read it slowly with new eyes; then read it out loud with new ears. Savor any word, phrase or concept that moves your heart. Ask God for the gifts of zeal and love to *know* Christ, to *experience* the power of his resurrection and, if you are up to it, even to *share* in his sufferings.

Faith-sharing

When your small group gathers for faith-sharing, use the above scripture passages which you have prayed with as the basis for your sharing. Refer to the suggestions in the Invitation if needed.

Small Group Exercises

1. Imagine yourself (or your group) sent by your parish or congregation to a small tribe of people who have never heard of Jesus. You know their language but you have absolutely no money. You also have only one year to be with them. How will you be with them? What will you say? What will you do?
2. Imagine that your pastor and any other ordained leaders are called away from your church indefinitely. How would the community operate? Be specific and try to list about twenty things your community would need and/or do. If a crisis came up, where would you turn? Would you write to your pastor? Why or why not?
3. Paul sometimes quotes "a saying of the Lord." What words of Jesus come to your mind often? Why? Do you ever use any of Jesus' sayings out loud? Why or why not?
4. Once Christians were taught to "prove" the resurrection, to "prove" Christ's divinity. But what we can prove we need no longer believe. What has faith meant to you over the years? How has the meaning of faith changed? Do you know any people whom you could describe as faith-filled? How do they act? How do you link beliefs *about* Jesus with belief *in* Jesus?
5. Return to a faith-sharing atmosphere. Take some quiet time to reflect on some beliefs *about* Jesus which are precious to you. Then share them with the group. Conclude with silent or spoken prayer for a deeper belief in, trust of, clinging to the person of Jesus.

Concluding Prayer

Leader:

> A reading from the prophet Isaiah.
> Do not be afraid, for I have called you by name. You are my own. I am your Love, your God, the Holy One, your deliverer. I give whole worlds for you. You are precious in my sight.... With tender affection I will bring you home.... My love shall be steady and shall never fail. My covenant of peace with you will never be shaken.
>
> The Word of the Lord.

All:

> Thanks be to God.

Leader:

> Our response to this reading is Psalm 139, with some silent questions for personal reflection.

Leader:

> Search me, O God, and know me.

Together:

> Know me as I sit or stand. I want you to read my innermost thoughts. I want you to know where I have been.

Silently:

> Remember some of your innermost feelings, desires, fantasies, actions, especially any you may never have brought to light before. Lay them open before God now.

Leader:

> You are precious in my sight.

Together:

> Before a word is on my lips, my Love, you know what I will say. You come so close to me, you are all around me on every side. I am overwhelmed by your presence, your understanding of me is so deep, beyond my grasp! Who can hide? I climb to the heavens you are there; I plunge to the depths and you are there. If I fly beyond the dawn or settle across the sea, you still have hold of me. You will be there to lead me. Your hand directs my whole life. Sometimes I think that night will hide me, that darkness will cover me.

Leader:

> You are precious in my sight.

All:

> Then darkness becomes bright as day. For you night shines like the day. Darkness and light are the same.

Leader:

> You are precious in my sight.

Together:

> You created every part of me, knitting me in my mother's womb. For such handiwork I praise you. This great wonder, the depth of my self, is awesome. You watched every bone in my body taking shape in secret, forming in the hidden depths. You saw my body grow according to your design.

Leader:

> You are precious in my sight.

Together:

> How deep are your thoughts and how vast! They are like countless grains of sand, far beyond my reach. Search my heart, probe me, and know my mind, Oh God. Lead me along your way. Amen.

2

John: A Sacramental Spirituality

The sun was setting, pouring a paint pot of color over the pines and one of the lakes of northern Minnesota. I stared open-mouthed and nudged my friend: "Isn't God good!" Her response shriveled me: "Why must you baptize everything?" Later, upon reflection, I realized what sacramental spirituality means for me. On that late afternoon, God was revealing truth and beauty everywhere I looked. I was not "baptizing" the scene, laying God-talk over the beauty. Rather, God's beauty seemed to leap out of creation, a revelation of God's sharing glory. Who could stem the flood or hold back the grandeur of God, which lights up and energizes the beauty of creation and the beauty of every person?

In such simple and ordinary experiences of God's glory, we know in our brains and our bones that the Spirit of God offers us God's life in and through Christ Jesus. If spirituality simply means our relationship with God, then a sacramental spirituality is a way of relating to God through every bit of creation. Creation both signals and embodies God's love for us. Sacramental spirituality sees-hears-smells-tastes-touches God's love in creation and perceives all of reality as God's revelation. Discovering *how* God comes close can be described as sacramental spirituality. This particular kind of incarnational spirituality characterizes the Fourth Gospel.

Questions

- ❧ What has been your own experience of sacrament and sacraments?
- ❧ What has been your experience of a sacramental spirituality, finding God in all things?

> In John's Gospel every created thing reveals God: wind and water, bread and wine, even conflict and cross. Where in the very earthy experiences of your life has God *revealed* and *been revealed?*

Scriptural Message

Deeper Meanings

John's Gospel is different from the other gospels of Matthew, Mark and Luke (called the synoptic gospels). For example, John's Gospel carries no story of Jesus' transfiguration on Mount Tabor. Why? Because Jesus is transfigured all through the Fourth Gospel. God's glory shines through his person, his work, his signs. In fact, scholars call the first twelve chapters of this gospel the Book of Signs. From his first sign in Cana, Jesus manifested his glory, and his disciples believed. His further signs also lead either to belief or to unbelief. All our gospels are invitations to participate in the living, loving, dying and resurrection of Jesus. Just as the original readers of the Fourth Gospel had to make their decision whether or not to believe and join Jesus, John's readers today, ourselves, are called to that same decision now: belief or unbelief.

Scholars may number Jesus' signs differently, but they agree that all these signs are life-giving. John himself points out the first two. The first is at the wedding in Cana (2: 1–11) where life and joy are symbolized by the gratuitous abundance of wine. The second is again at Cana (4: 46–54), where the official's son is healed by the power of Jesus' word which is life (6: 63, 68).

In chapter five, again with a word, Jesus heals, frees and restores to wholeness of life (wholeness being the literal Greek word) the paralytic who has been lying trapped by the pool for thirty-eight years (5: 2–9). Feeding the multitude, which is a miracle of multiplying bread in the synoptic gospels, is transformed by John's sacramental spirituality into a deeper sign of life, of food for eternal life, a food and drink which is Jesus himself (6: 27, 33, 35-40, 51, 54). Although in the synoptic gospels Jesus heals various blind people, his healing the man born blind in chapter nine is really more a symbolic life-and-light-giving touch than just a mere physical cure. Martha's confession of faith that Jesus is the resurrection and life precedes the sign of Lazarus' life restored, a sign that drew crowds (12: 18) and threatened some Jewish leaders.

While all Jesus' signs point to and actually confer life, it is the Lazarus-back-to-life sign which ironically sets the machinery in motion for the death of the life-giver, the ultimate sign of his being lifted up. "This man does many signs" (11: 47), his enemies note. More than *doing* signs, this man *is* the sign.

The second part of John's Gospel is the Book of Glory. It begins with chapter thirteen's scene of the foot-washing, a sign of God's ministry to us. The one who will be lifted up first kneels before us. When Jesus is lifted up on the cross, not so much in pain as in exaltation, he himself becomes the sign par excellence of God's love and fidelity in all its fullness. John's community offers us all Jesus' signs, especially his dying and exaltation, so we may believe and thus have eternal life. Then, we are promised, our joy will be full (cf. 1 Jn 1: 4).

Transforming Power

The entire life and work, death and resurrection of Jesus was sacramental for John and his community — sacramental because Jesus' touch and word were transforming, grace-filled, life-giving, God's glory poured out. In John's Gospel, Jesus' signs are much more than the prophetic signs which we read about in the Jewish scriptures. Prophetic signs *point* to God at work. Jesus' signs do more. They *embody* God's life, they do what they symbolize. Each sign in the Fourth Gospel is "a material action pointing toward a spiritual reality," says scripture scholar Raymond Brown. These signs also point to the time after Jesus' death and resurrection when living water (7: 37-39) and living bread (6: 53-59), fresh sight

(9: 141) and new movement (5: 2–14) will be available to us in abundance.

In John's Gospel, signs are also symbols, carrying many meanings. For us, symbols are rich, not only offering insight and understanding but also evoking our memories and imaginations, sparking our emotions and hungers, spurring our decisions and work. Theologian Bernard Cooke writes that symbols express "our most personal and important and disturbing experiences." Not only do they express us at a deep level, but they are "a powerful force in shaping the way we think and feel ... the fact that we are embodied spirits means that we exist symbolically." John's sacramental spirituality then is an embodied, incarnational spirituality.

The word "true" threads through John's Gospel. Sometimes it means the Hebrew word "faithful," but most often it means the Greek "really real." The evangelist proclaims the true light (1: 9), the true bread (6: 32), the true vine (15: 1) underlying every light, all food and each growing thing in this world: Jesus. What is real food? Jesus' flesh. What is real drink? Jesus' blood (6: 55). All other food and drink are shadows. All shepherds point to the true shepherd, all water indicates living, welling-up water, all wine reminds us of the messianic banquet.

The temple in Jerusalem is a symbol of the true temple, the body of Christ (2: 18–21). True worship is neither in temple nor in shrine, not on certain mountains (4: 23–24) nor in special rites, but in Christ's body. The serpent lifted up by Moses in the desert offers temporary healing compared with the deeper, complete healing which Jesus effects when he is lifted up on the cross (3: 14–15). The bridegroom image, which the prophets of Israel used to symbolize God's love and fidelity, is enfleshed in Jesus, the true bridegroom (3: 29). The real grain of wheat, which falls into the ground, dies, and brings forth much fruit, is Jesus himself (12: 24). All death, all grain, all blossoming are to point to the deeper reality, our call to share in Jesus' living, dying and bearing fruit. As for us, John calls us to be true worshipers (4: 23) and true disciples (8: 31), to be what we really are.

John's is the only gospel to portray Jesus' side opened on the cross, pouring forth blood and water, symbols of baptism and Eucharist (19: 34). Not only are baptism and Eucharist primary sacraments, but every creature is a sacrament, filled with the glory of God.

Daily Contemplation

How can we begin or continue to foster a sacramental spirituality? If we are "Greek in spirit," we will want to see, to pay attention. The Greeks came to the disciples saying, "We want to see Jesus" (Jn 12: 20). We can pay attention to the beauty around us, notice the tiny indications of God at work, look beyond the obvious, contemplate what the poet Gerard Manley Hopkins phrased the "dearest freshness deep down things." A sacramental spirituality invites us to contemplate mystery.

"How were your eyes opened?" asked the neighbors of the man born blind (9: 10). With this kind of contemplation, surely a gift from God, we can sit with one flower for fifteen minutes, we can rest our spirit in looking at a twenty-minute sunset, we can gaze at a sleeping baby for half an hour. We can let our imaginations, memories, intuitions, hopes and fears draw us into the beauty, the truth which God always and everywhere is revealing.

If we are "Hebrew in spirit," our mode of contemplation might better be hearing. We can hear beyond the obvious, like sheep who recognize the voice of their own true shepherd among all the competing voices (10: 1–5). "Everyone who is of the truth hears my voice," Jesus says (18: 37). Mary of Magdala in the garden on Easter morning is a model of paying attention to the voice of Jesus. It is "still dark" until Jesus reveals himself with a word. "Mary," the risen Lord calls (20: 1, 16). She recognizes his voice, even in the dark.

Hearing, seeing, touching, tasting, smelling, feeling, intuiting, thinking, choosing, wanting, remembering, imagining — all aspects of our humanness, our bodiliness — lead us to a sacramental spirituality, to embrace a world set afire with the glory of God. John the evangelist portrays bodily elements, all creation as signs to reveal and communicate divine realities. All life is a sacrament.

John draws on powerful cultural images, both Hebrew and Greek, to express some of who Jesus is. Light, water, bread, fountains, lambs, wine, rabbis, shepherds — all can image the Sign of God in our world. Our evangelist looks beyond vines and shepherds and lights and bread to see the true vine, the real shepherd, the total light, the true bread. If we, in response to the good news of God's coming close and revealing glory in all of creation, can be open to God's self-communication, be alert to everything in human life and creation which "signs" God, we are fostering a sacramental spirituality.

Awe characterizes the one who prays out of a sacramental spirituality. This wonder-full kind of response to God did not just begin with the coming of Christ, however. The community of Israel, too, knew that God could come close in so many ways. One of their favorite images of God's nearness is the true shepherd. Of all the images we could select from the Fourth Gospel to pray with, we focus first on this image of shepherd, which John's community must often have pondered in their hearts.

Guided Prayer Passages

Ezekiel 34: 11–16

> The Lord speaks: I myself will go after my sheep ... and rescue them no matter where they were scattered on dark and cloudy days.... I will lead them home to their own soil. I will graze them on the mountains of Israel, by streams and in all the green fields. I myself will tend my flock. I will search for the lost, recover the straggler, bandage the hurt,

strengthen the sick, set the strong and healthy out to play, and give them all their proper food.

Notice how the good shepherd crafts his care to the need of each sheep. He pays close attention to each in order to give each what is most helpful and healthful. This shepherd contemplates each creature in his care. Here, God is imaged as the one who first contemplates us, and our contemplation of the true shepherd flows in response to God's loving gaze at us.

Sacramental spirituality helps us to be strong and healthy. In John's Gospel we see that God sends Jesus so that we may have life, and not just enough life to get by, but life in abundance (10: 10).

God passionately desires that we be strong and healthy, and so be set out to play. When, in our loss and weariness and pain, we neglect God's hope for us, God the Good Shepherd comes close to gather us in, gather us up, and heal us so that we may romp again in the pastures.

Ask God to heal you of any negative images of God, of any fears you may have in letting God come close, fears of whatever might be twisted in your spirituality, your relationship with God. Gaze on God who gazes on you and sees to your every need tenderly.

Psalm 80

> Hear us, O shepherd of Israel, you who lead us.
>
> Show yourself to us. Rouse up your power and come.
> Restore us, O God. Show yourself to us.
> Let your face shine upon us and we will be saved.
> Show yourself to us. You brought a vine out of Egypt.
> You planted it, clearing the ground before it.
> Your vine took deep root and filled the land.
> The mountains were covered with its shade.

> O Lord, remember your vine and tend it. Grant us new life. Lord, show yourself to us. Let your face shine upon us, and we will be saved.

The early Church probably applied this psalm to Jesus who was loved as Good Shepherd, God's tender care in the flesh. John's Gospel also calls Jesus our true vine, one who was planted deep in this earth, who took his nourishment from the earth and elements, and who in turn, now as risen Lord, nourishes us, his branches. Re-pray the psalm with gratitude that God's face now shines on us through the glorious face of Jesus.

John 2: 1–11

> On the third day there was a wedding in Cana of Galilee and the mother of Jesus was there. Both Jesus and his disciples were invited to the wedding. When the wine ran out, the mother of Jesus said to him: "They have no wine." Jesus said to her: "What difference does that make to you and me, woman? My hour has not yet come." His mother said to the servants: "Whatever he tells you to do, do it."
>
> Now there were six stone water jars there, in accordance with the purification rites of the Jews. Each could contain twenty to thirty gallons of water. Jesus said to the servants: "Fill the jars with water." They filled them to the top.
>
> He said to them: "Now draw and carry some to the master of this feast." They did, and when the master had tasted the water made wine, he did not know from where it had come. The servants knew. So the master of the feast called the bridegroom and said: "Everyone sets out the best wine first. Then when guests become drunk, the host puts out the worse wine. You have kept the good wine till now."
>
> Now this which Jesus did in Cana of Galilee was the beginning of the signs. These signs showed forth his glory, and his disciples believed in him.

Some eighteen-hundred years later, the Jesuit poet Gerard Manley Hopkins expressed what the disciples must have felt at Cana when Jesus "first manifested his glory" (2: 11). He wrote: "The world is charged with the grandeur of God.... There lives the dearest freshness deep down things."

The disciples experienced not just an extravaganza of wine that they could smell and touch and taste. They felt that transcendent glory which lit up their experience from within, the "dearest freshness deep down things." And yet they saw darkly. Only after the resurrection, could they see everywhere, "It is the Lord!" (21: 7).

What sacraments do you find in your daily living, loving and work? Name certain holy places in your life. What material objects point you toward God? What music leads you to contemplate? What brings sudden tears to your eyes? What surprises you with joy? What causes you open-mouthed wonder?

John 2: 13–21

The Passover of the Jews drew near, and Jesus went up to Jerusalem. In the temple he found men selling oxen, sheep and doves, and others dealing coins. Having made a whip out of ropes, he threw the sheep and oxen out of the temple and, turning over the tables of the money-changers, he poured out their coins. To those selling doves Jesus said: "Take these things out of here. Do not make the house of my Father a house of trade."

Now his disciples remembered that it had been written: "Zeal for your house will consume me." The Jews reacted and said to Jesus: "What sign do you show us, that you can do things like this?" Jesus answered them: "Destroy this shrine and in three days I will raise it." So the Jews said: "Forty-six years it took to build this shrine and you will raise it up in three days?" But Jesus was speaking about the shrine of his body.

The human body, of Jesus, once rooted in earth, is the true temple, the most real and most holy place of worship. What is our culture's attitude toward the human body? What is the attitude of official Church teaching? What is your attitude toward the human body? Your own body? How do you imagine that the evangelist and the community who shaped John's Gospel came to revere Jesus' flesh as the holy place of true worship? Ask them. Then ask Jesus to form and re-form your attitudes toward your body, senses and emotions so as to conform with his attitudes and actions.

John 21: 4–12

> Just as the dawn was breaking, Jesus stood on the lakeshore. His disciples, however, did not know that it was Jesus. Jesus said to them, "Children, have you any fish?" They answered, "No." So Jesus said, "Cast the net on the right side of the boat and you will find some." So they threw out the net and then were unable to drag in the huge number of fish. The disciple whom Jesus loved said to Peter, "It is the Lord!" ... When they got out of the boat on the beach, they saw a coal fire, with fish lying on it, and some bread.... Jesus said to them, "Come and have breakfast."

A sacramental spirituality recognizes the Lord in everything: "It is the Lord!" Sometimes we encounter the risen Christ during prayer or public worship, but sometimes we find him in the most unusual places — like cooking breakfast on the beach, or washing feet. Ask yourself: Who cares for you, serves you, even in some small way? How is that person Christ for you? Spirituality is not just about our loving God but also about letting God, and others, love us.

When and where have you discovered Christ's service to you? If it is easy to recognize Christ's presence in a huge quantity of fish or blessing or whatever we need, how do you recognize his presence in the ordinary, in daily events, in setback, in lack and in pain?

Finding God in all things both flows from and nourishes gratitude as well as a contemplative, sacramental spirituality. Ask God for this grace: to notice, to recognize and to cry often today: "It is the Lord!"

John 21: 4–12 (above)

Today read this passage aloud. Then imagine the scene as vividly as possible. Smell the water, the fish, etc. Do you identify more with Peter or with the one whom Jesus loved? Do you recognize Jesus in your life? Do you "jump in" at once just to be with him — or are you hesitant to get close to him? He wants to feed you, to serve you. How do you feel about that? Tell him.

John 21: 4–12 (above)

Recall when, during this week, you were able to say, "It's the Lord!" How were you able to recognize him? Did your heart tell you? Did you know him in joy? In pain? In anger? In being with your husband/wife, community? In caring for a friend? In laughing with your children? In feeling the rebirth of creation? In being forgiven? How is the Lord evident to you? Ask the Spirit to show or to speak Jesus to you, in yourself and in others.

John 1: 14, 16–18

> The Word became flesh and pitched his tent among us, and we saw his glory ... full of grace and truth.... And out of his fullness we have all received, grace upon grace upon grace upon grace. The law came through Moses, but grace and truth have come through Jesus Christ. Now no one has ever seen God, but the one who is closest to God's own heart has made God known.

The translation: "grace upon grace upon grace upon grace" tries to capture the meaning of the Greek word for "upon." This preposition in Greek means never-ending. Ask Jesus to remind you when you have received grace upon grace upon grace. Jesus reveals God. Ask him to remind you of people, things, events, incidents that have revealed God to you. God continues to take flesh in our day. God is incarnate in us and in our brothers and sisters. Bring into your mind, one by one, each relative, friend and acquaintance, and look on them with as much love as you would look at Jesus. Thank and praise God who takes flesh in each one, grace upon grace upon grace upon grace.

Faith-sharing

When your small group gathers for faith-sharing, use the above scripture passages which you have prayed over as the basis for your sharing. Refer to the suggestions in the Invitation if needed.

Small Group Exercises

1. *Baptizo* in Greek means to be immersed in. To be baptized into Christ means to be plunged into him, immersed in him. How did you think of baptism when you were a child? Did the meaning of baptism change for you over the years? Why? How?
2. Some results which flow from our baptism are: immersion in Christ; forgiveness of sin; becoming the body of Christ, inclusion in the Church community; the source of God's life within us; putting on the mind and heart of Christ ... and more. Which of the above speaks to your experience? Why?

Concluding Prayer

Leader:

Let us slowly and thoughtfully pray together Psalm 80.

Together:

Hear us, Oh shepherd of Israel, you who lead us.
Show yourself to us. Rouse up your power and come.
Restore us, O God. Show yourself to us.
Let your face shine upon us and we will be saved.
Show yourself to us. You brought a vine out of Egypt.
You planted it, clearing the ground before it.
Your vine took deep root and filled the land.
The mountains were covered with its shade.
Oh Lord, remember your vine and tend it.
Grant us new life. Lord, show yourself to us.
Let your face shine upon us and we will be saved.

Part II

Jesus as Sacrament of God and Our Response to God's Sharing Glory

Jesus as Sacrament

As sacrament, the tangible experience of God, Jesus is central to the New Testament. Both Paul and John and their communities knew Jesus. Some knew him in the flesh, but all knew him through their religious experience of him as the risen Christ, the way to union with God. Although there are many titles for Christ by which the early Church tried to convey their worship and love for him, we will attend to Paul's and John's writings concerning only four:

- *the Word of Life*
- *the dying and resurrected one*
- *the disciple and apostle of God*
- *the bread of life.*

By keeping our eyes fixed on Jesus (Heb 12: 1–2) we are contemplating. To study Jesus as he was in relationship to the members of the first Christian communities is to relate with him alive today.

The Human Situation: Grace and Sin

Preaching in the early Church had two aims. First, preaching proclaimed the good news of all that God had done to heal, reconcile and renew the human family in Christ Jesus. Then, the first Christian preachers exhorted their listeners to respond to God by turning away from sin and receiving the fullness of God's grace through the indwelling of the Holy Spirit.

In chapters three to six, we will keep our eyes fixed on Jesus, our sure way to union with God. Then we will listen to God's desire to replace our sin with grace. We will consider ourselves and our human situation.

3

Jesus, Word of Life

Questions

- What is your favorite title for Jesus? What is your experience of Jesus? Knowing, trusting, loving, responding to him?
- What has been your experience of Jesus in your parish or community?
- Where have you discovered him? In people? In liturgy? In other sacraments? In the leaders? In parish or community events?

Scriptural Message

Paul

Jesus is central to Paul's life, his thinking, choosing, loving, feeling. All Paul wants, he writes, is to know Christ Jesus (Phil 3: 8). His entire energy, it seems, is spent probing the mystery of Christ, coming to know him ever more deeply, more intimately. For a Hebrew, to know means so much more than apprehending with the intellect. It means to be "intimately united with," a verb used in Hebrew even for the act of sexual intercourse. Instead of closing down his mind and heart before the great mystery of Christ, Paul wants to remain open to the mystery. Mystery calls for our continual contemplation and ever more conscious, free surrender. Paul is always engaged with the mystery of Christ.

Paul met the risen Lord on the road to Damascus in a powerful religious experience. Although our experience of Jesus as risen or as Lord will probably not be as dramatic as Paul's, real religious experience is possible for all of us. We, too, keep asking Jesus, "Who are you?" and year by year the answer varies, as we come to know him and respond to him more completely

Paul never met Jesus in the flesh or talked to him face to face. If he had known the historical Jesus, eaten supper with him, talked far into the night with him, worshiped with him in the temple, laughed at his jokes, managed the crowds for him, then Paul could have returned to their shared history in his preaching. He could have spoken of "the good old days" when he and Jesus traveled together. Instead, Paul wants to know Jesus in the Hebrew way, a knowing which leads to loving trust and deep union. Paul knows, not by fact, verifiable data, historical memories, but by faith.

For Paul, faith in Jesus the risen Lord means that he cannot rely on any first-hand fact or memory but has to trust the religious experience with which God has graced him. God has introduced Paul to the risen Lord, and Paul's faith means trusting God's love, God's revelation of who God is in Christ Jesus.

Faith for Paul does not mean "intellectual assent to divinely revealed truths." Faith means knowing a person and surrendering in love and trust to that person. For Paul, faith means clinging to Jesus. Those words may annoy or distance some of us who prefer a more rational, less intimate definition of faith. Yet Karl Rahner, a theologian with one of the most stellar intellects of our time, invites us to have "the courage to throw our arms about him." For Paul and for us, being "in Christ" is our very life. Faith, our attachment to Christ, both gives and deepens our life.

John

The Fourth Gospel, too, is about faith and life. It is especially about Christ, the very life of God made flesh. John's community has written a gospel full of signs, so that we might believe and thus have life in Jesus the Christ (Jn 20: 30–31). All the signs which this community will reflect on and eventually record are expressions of divine life, life in abundance. The Fourth Gospel itself is an expression of life. The Word of Life, the gospel, is a sacrament.

John's community, even after the gospel was written, continued to be shaped by the Word of Life, a word which for the author of the First Epistle of John was very tangible, "in the flesh."

> That which was from the beginning, what we have heard, what we have seen with our eyes, what we have looked upon and touched with our hands is the very Word of Life. This Life was made visible, and we have seen, we witness, we proclaim to you this eternal Life who was with the Father and manifested to us. We announce this which we have seen and heard to you so that you may have communion with us. Our union is with the Father and with the Son, Jesus Christ. We write this so that our joy might be completely full. (1 Jn 1: 1–4)

It is not just that the words of Jesus are spirit and life. Jesus himself is the Word of Life. When God speaks the Word Jesus, life abounds. In many and diverse ways, the author of Hebrews writes, God tried to communicate with us (Heb 1: 1–2). God tried to lavish on us, through the lives of our spiritual ancestors, all that God has to give (Rom 8: 32). God spoke to that people again and again. Finally God speaks Jesus. That Word takes flesh, and in a wonderful image in the original Greek, pitches his tent among us.

> The Word was made flesh and pitched his tent among us ... Out of his fullness we have all received grace upon grace upon grace. The law came through Moses, but grace and truth have come through Jesus Christ. (Jn 1: 14, 16–17)

The law, God's revelation and covenant word with Israel, was given through Moses. It was God's self-expression. However, the Fourth Gospel proclaims, grace and truth have come through Jesus

Christ. What God had been trying to communicate, reveal, lavish on the people of Israel was not doctrine, not even truths, but grace, God's own self. Grace is God's free gift of love. Grace in the scriptures is linked with truth, which is God's fidelity to us. God's grace and truth *(hesed* and *'emet* in the Hebrew language) are most characteristic of God. God's *hesed* and *'emet* have come and continue to come to us through Jesus Christ.

Just as God is mystery, never to be defined, so it is hard to find words to translate these two Hebrew words which characterize God. *Hesed* (grace) means God's extravagant, abundant, unconditional love, mercy, kindness and tenderness. *'Emet* (truth) means God's unswerving, sure, true, everlasting fidelity.

In the New Testament, *hesed* and *'emet* express Jesus who is among us as God's own self. They are translated as compassion and faithfulness to characterize Jesus, just as once these words described God in the Jewish scriptures.

Some of the religious leaders of Jesus' time and the time of John's community could not hear this "Word" of God's kindness and faithfulness. Like Paul before his conversion, they simply could not receive the word of grace, the *hesed* and *'emet* of God. They felt that they had to work at their spirituality, earn their holiness, study scripture so that they could find the right answers. Jesus accuses them:

> You search the scriptures because you think that in them you have eternal life. It is they that bear witness to me, yet you refuse to come to me that you may have life. (Jn 5: 39–40)

We search the scriptures not to become more certain of doctrines, more holy, more able to prove points in an argument. We study and pray with scripture in order to come to Jesus himself for life. Indeed, the scriptures mediate life. The word of God in law and prophets and psalms, in gospels and epistles, is a sacrament. Scripture is a sacrament, which both reveals God's life and engages us in that life. As we hear in Isaiah 55, God's word accomplishes the purpose for which it is sent. If the word of scripture tells of healing, then even as we read we are being healed. If the word describes the passing through the Red Sea, it is we who are being led to freedom today.

In John's Gospel, the Word of Life does what it says. It nourishes (6: 33); it heals (5: 8–9); it cleanses (15: 3); it enlightens (9: 6–7); it enlivens (11: 43); it judges (12: 48). If we make the word (scripture) our home, the Word (Jesus) makes us his disciples, teaches us truth and sets us free (8: 31–32). We believe that water and oil, bread and wine, words of absolution and words of commitment, hands on heads, and fingers anointing senses, actually do what they signify. And so we believe the word of God accomplishes what God sends it to do (Is 55). Both the Jewish and the Christian scriptures are tangible, concrete signs of God's life at work among us. Scripture is a sacrament.

If we listen to the word of God, we will hear a call to obey. (The Latin root of "obey" is *ab audire*, meaning "to hear.") To obey does not mean conformity or adherence to law. It means to hear God's word with our whole being, to let the Word of God take flesh in us. In the Fourth Gospel, Jesus describes his own obedience as eating, drinking and being nourished by the will of God (4: 34).

To hear and obey is what John means by believing. Believing is a kind of knowing God. Knowing God is not the same as knowing divinely revealed truths. Knowing God, and the one whom God sent, is eternal life (17: 3). Like Paul's understanding of faith as attachment, this life-giving kind of knowing means belonging, a mutual commitment to one another: "The one who belongs to God hears the words of God" (8: 47). Both John and Paul thus understand faith as a mutual indwelling, God in us and we in Christ, a mutual commitment and attachment between God/Jesus/ Spirit and ourselves.

To hear the Word of God is to be a disciple. *(Discipulus, discipula* in Latin means "pupil or learner.") To learn continually from God, from Jesus, from the Spirit of truth is to be a disciple. We will always be learning more about the mystery of God. Mystery, Karl Rahner defines, is that which is "infinitely knowable." That is, for all eternity we will be knowing God, discovering "beauty ever ancient, ever new." How important, then, to make our home in the word of scripture, to be at home in the Word made flesh. In Christ we continually learn, and gradually the Spirit deepens our discipleship.

For the Jews of Jesus' time, to study scripture was to worship. In the Jewish milieu knowing God never meant simply intellectual apprehension of God, but wholehearted union with God. To receive and ponder, to wonder and digest the word of God was a way to be united with God through the sign, the sacrament of scripture. As we proceed in our prayerful study of Paul's letters and John's Gospel, we are worshiping together. We are, through this study, coming to know and be united with the "one true God and the one whom God sent" (Jn 17: 3) in a deeper and fuller way. This, Jesus promises us, is eternal life, union — now. We do not have to wait for eternity to become engaged with this Mystery. We can know and be deeply united with God now. For as Paul asserts, we are *in Christ,* not later in heaven, but now in the midst of our daily dealings and delights.

Guided Prayer Passages

Isaiah 55: 10–11

> Just as rain and snow come from the heavens, watering the earth, bringing forth fruit, giving seed to those who sow and bread to those who eat, so my word will not return empty. It goes forth from my mouth and accomplishes what I want.

God's word is powerful and does what it says, accomplishing all that God wants. Sacraments do what they signify, too. How did you define sacrament when you were younger? How would you describe sacrament, now that you have had more experience of sacraments? How can "scripture as sacrament" fit your former definition of sacrament? How can it fit your current and experiential description?

From Psalm 19

> The heavens tell the glory of God,
> and their music speeds through all the earth.
> In the heavens a tent is fixed for the sun who comes out rejoicing like one newly wed.
> The word of the Lord refreshes our spirits.
> The Lord's word makes the simple wise.
> The word of the Lord rejoices the heart.
> The word shines clear and abides forever.
> God's word is more precious than gold,
> sweeter than syrup or honey from the comb.

The Word in this psalm is the same Word who was made flesh — and, rejoicing like one newlywed, pitches his tent among us. Image the risen Lord as the Sun, like a newly wed, rejoicing in the heavens. Image the same Word in darkness: "When all things were in quiet stillness, your Word, full of power, leapt down" (Wis 18: 14–15). Do you experience yourself right now as more in light or in darkness? Invite the Word to come close.

John 8: 31–32

> If you make my word your home, you will be my disciples. You will know the truth and the truth will set you free.

In the other three New Testament gospels, discipleship means following Jesus. John's Gospel, however, is faithful to the Latin meaning of disciple as learner. From your own experience of being a disciple, what do you think being a disciple entails?

Ask the Spirit to call to your mind some things that you have learned from God. How has the truth you have learned, not necessarily from books but in prayer, helped to set you free? Try to be very concrete in your memories and write them down. In this writing you are involved in much the same process as an evangelist: recording your experience of God's living word in your life. To remember, to study, to read your own recorded memories is to worship the God who communicates with you.

John 17: 3

> This is eternal life — to know you, the one true faithful God and the one whom God has sent.

Take five minutes of silence to ponder this one verse. To study, to know, to worship, to be in union. When, where, how have you experienced union with God even as you listened to or read or studied the Word in scripture or in theology? Did a Sunday sermon awaken your heart? Was it a spiritual book or a novel? In loving union with a person? On a retreat? A film? Let your memory stay with that experience. What feelings arise in you? Share those feelings with God/Jesus/Spirit. Share what you choose of these incidents and feelings with a friend or with your group.

John 15: 16, 13

> You did not choose me. I chose you that you may bear fruit.... Greater love has no one than to lay down his or her life for a friend.

If the Word is to continue to take flesh in us today, if our knowing God is to bear fruit, then our growth in obedience means our gradual growth in action, laying down our lives in some small way for our brothers and sisters. Don't make a resolution about this. Ask simply to be open to God's choosing you, day after day. To deepen your discipleship, be silent and ask the Spirit of truth to teach you today some way in which you can offer a small, perhaps even hidden, act of love to another.

Faith-sharing

When your small group gathers for faith-sharing, use the above scripture passages which you have prayed over as the basis for your sharing. Refer to the suggestions in the Invitation if needed.

Small Group Exercise

After three to four minutes of silent reflection, brainstorm about any area of your parish, community, neighborhood, city, country or world where people need truth and freedom. Let one or two word responses just flow from each member, without any comment. Have someone jot down every idea, even "wild" ones. There are no right or wrong or smarter or holier ideas — just promptings of the Spirit of truth.

Concluding Prayer

After the flow of ideas in the exercise above dwindles, let the leader ask aloud for the Spirit's guidance. Then let the note-taker slowly read everything back to the group. After each idea, let the group respond with this prayer:

Together:

> Mercy on your people, Lord.

During the week, let these areas of concern, these needy people, float in and out of your consciousness and prayer. Thank and praise God for calling you, however gradually, to action.

4

Jesus, the Dying-Resurrected One

Questions:

- What has been your personal devotion to the crucified Jesus over the years?
- How would you describe it now?
- What has been our Church's devotion over the centuries? How would you describe it now?

That God had raised Jesus from the dead was the central theme of the first Christian preaching. Very exciting and good news to a desperate, despairing Greco-Roman society. Very exciting and good news to a Jewish society, which looked for the end time when the reign of God would break in with the resurrection of all the dead. This Good News is what Christians proclaimed: the end time has arrived.

- What impact has Jesus' resurrection on today's society?
- On your parish's or community's life? On your life?
- If the impact is little or nothing, what can you do to "preach" that Jesus is alive?

Scriptural Message

Paul

God's love and life were totally poured out in the dying and raising of Jesus, which is the source of our salvation, our reconciliation, our freedom. How is it that Paul and his communities could return again and again to that mystery for constant rejoicing, gratitude, wonder, nourishment? Faced with the same mystery, many of us are left unmoved: "That's just history," or, "Jesus is dead and gone, so what's the difference?" But the contrary is true! Our faith testifies that Jesus lives, and that his history is *now*, entwined with our own histories.

The dying and raising of Jesus is meant to be the central story of our Christian lives, the major movement in the worship of our lives. It is *the* mystery of faith, the core of the gospels, what we celebrate at Eucharist. It is the meaning of baptism, the reason we are community, sister and brother to each other.

And we need both the dying and the raising. If the crucifixion is not rooted in human history, then we can drift off into the ethereal fantasy that we are only an Alleluia people. On the other hand, if Christ is not raised as Paul wrote, then our faith, our clinging to him, our commitment to him is in vain. Our relationship with him would be illusion. The dying and resurrection of Jesus are inseparable.

In our modern culture, which claims to be Christian, there seems to be a lack of interest in the crucifixion and resurrection. In both society and Church, we seem much more preoccupied with morality.

It seems that so many of us first-world Christians tend to ignore the great news of God's love totally poured out in the dying and raising of Jesus. Three partial reasons for this apparent gap in our communal faith and our contemporary preaching may be our fear of powerlessness, our denial of death, and our denial of sin.

Fear of powerlessness

The cross is the ultimate symbol of powerlessness. Just as Paul's first-century hearers, many of us find the cross of Christ both a stumbling block and foolishness (1 Cor 1: 23). Many in the Corinthian community were enchanted by miracles worked by various Christian preachers who came after Paul. Paul names these opponents of his "super-apostles" (2 Cor 11: 5). The Corinthians, like some of us today who run after spectacular visions or healings, were quite unimpressed by Paul, who only wanted to preach Christ and him crucified. We, too, might prefer to be associated with the powerful, miracle-working Son of God rather than with the sweaty, tormented man stumbling on the way to Calvary. Many times, Christians would rather focus on a belief in Jesus as God rather than the human Jesus who was so powerless.

Our need to concentrate on Jesus' divinity and wonder-working powers may stem from fear or even hatred of what we perceive as weakness in ourselves, in our leaders and/or even in our God. How could Jesus, the very embodiment of God, embrace this powerlessness, emptying himself for death on a cross (Phil 2: 8)? We, contrary to Jesus, hurry to build up our spiritual and social credentials, our store of merit and grace, as well as wealth and power and fame. No wonder the frightened yet willing man of Nazareth, staggering out of control toward crucifixion, is such a stumbling block.

Denial of Death

Many of us do not want to ponder death in our hearts. Not Jesus', not our own. *Denial of Death* by Ernest Becker won the Pulitzer Prize in 1974. This book exposes our culture's refusal to accept our finite creaturehood. Becker pinpoints our efforts to escape death, but in so doing, he asserts, we miss life. We moderns numb ourselves with TV, alcohol, shopping, drugs, work. We delude ourselves by thinking that we control outer space and inner space, the human body and psyche. Yet we feel pushed out of control by computer technology, by bureaucracy, by a rising suicide rate, by natural disasters. Instead of the eager expectation of the end of time and space that Paul encouraged in his communities, we dread a self-inflicted destruction of the world, and bury our dread and helplessness in personal and societal depression.

"Who can save us from this body of death?" Paul asks this question in his letter to the Romans and answers it as we would expect: Jesus Christ (Rom 7: 24–25). Jesus Christ alone can save us from death. Jesus Christ crucified in weakness, Paul might add. Jesus the loser, Jesus who understands in his very gut our human temptation to deny our own mortality. Jesus deeply understands our flight from pain, both physical and emotional. He knows our hopelessness in the face of unjust political and religious structures.

In obedience Jesus accepted these terrors; therefore, God could transform him in the midst of them. God raised Jesus from fear and helplessness, from failure and mortality. Jesus' resurrection is our hope. God's power promises us the same transformation of our own failure, powerlessness and pain. Jesus is the first-born of the new creation, the first-born of many brothers and sisters. This is why Paul exults, "Death, where is your victory? Death, where is your sting?" (1 Cor 15: 55).

For Paul this dying and raising was such good news. As a Pharisee, he believed that resurrection from the dead was the primary sign of God's reign breaking into the created universe, into the human heart. Because Jesus was raised from the dead, Paul realized that the eschatological event was begun. ("Eschatological" simply means the experience of the end time, the last things: death, judgment, heaven, hell.) The end of the world was beginning with the first One born into new life, the risen Christ.

With great urgency, Paul preached the dying/resurrected Christ: "For he was crucified in weakness but lives by the power of God" (2 Cor 13: 4). While we may fear the end of the world in our day, in Paul's time it offered hope to believers. Most of them were oppressed by the economy, by slavery and violence as well as by pagan religions, which emphasized capricious gods and oracles. Paul believed that God who had raised Jesus would soon send the Lord Jesus on the clouds of heaven to gather the chosen into God's kingdom (1 Thes 5: 1–11). How eagerly Paul invited people to be baptized, immersed into the dying of Jesus so that the new and risen life of Jesus could become apparent in their mortal flesh (2 Cor 4: 10–11). Paul concludes his first letter to the

Corinthians with the familiar early Christian cry of longing: "Our Lord, come!" (1 Cor 16: 22; see also Rev 22: 17).

Denial of Sin

Skimming over the depths of the crucifixion may indicate not only our fear of powerlessness and death but also our denial of sin, for Jesus' crucifixion reveals our sin: "Death, where is your sting? The sting of death is sin" (1 Cor 15: 55–56). When God's love has been completely em-bodied in the man on the cross, completely spent for us, then grace lights up our darkness, uncovers our sin. Paul asks us to believe that when we were God's enemies, Christ died for us (Rom 5: 10). We call crucifixion day *Good* Friday because of this incredibly good news. Instead of a tyrant-god who will crush us in our sins, the God of Jesus and of Paul loves us, even in our hostility toward God.

In today's secular society we Christians can trivialize sin, that sin which has called forth such great love. We tend to dismiss our sinning, our malice and rebellion, our weakness and pettiness with, "Oh, God won't care." On the contrary, God cares so passionately that Jesus poured out his whole life for us. Hanging on that cross, Jesus attracted every evil, every weakness of the human heart and human society. In absorbing all that evil, he broke the cycle of evil by refusing to pass it on. He killed the power of sin in his obedient, forgiving person. Paul knew that the crucified Jesus once and for all broke the power of sin and death in his own death.

The cross, revealing such lavish love and life, also reveals our sin, for the ground of our hearts has been plowed up by "the human condition": all the rejections, losses and deprivations we have suffered. Sin has its root in this human condition, which Jesus embraced. "He was made sin for us," Paul cryptically states (2 Cor 5: 21), so "that we might be made the very goodness of God." Theologian John Shea describes Jesus' work with sinners and the sinned against: "To the rejected, he became an event of inclusion; to the envious he became an event of unmasking. To the bereft he became a banquet; to the self-righteous a mirror."

Yet, besides revealing love and sin, the cross joins the resurrection in revealing God's power. For Paul and for two thousand years of Christian experience, the joined dying and resurrection of Jesus has been the central and most extravagantly loving act of God on behalf of humankind. This act most totally embodies God's gift of self to us in Jesus, and unleashes the source of all spiritual life into the human heart and into human society. This source is the Spirit.

John

God's Will

How can the cruel death of Jesus be God's extravagantly loving act? For some of us not only denial of death, sin, or powerlessness provoke us to shy away from the cross, but the possibility that God's will may mean suffering and death makes us quickly look away. And understandably so. Who would want God close when we see what God "did" to Jesus, such a good and innocent man? An image of "satisfaction" — that God required Jesus' torture and bloody death to atone for the heinous sins of humankind — has colored one thousand years of spirituality, and we sometimes still struggle with the concept today.

However, the recent renewal of scripture study has begun to reveal a more balanced view of God with regard to Jesus' death. True, we see Jesus sweating blood in Gethsemane, so afraid of death that he could have suffered a panic attack. Then we hear him surrender: "Not my will but yours be done" (Mk 14: 36). So what happens next may seem to be God's will. His betrayer kisses him, his friends abandon him, his torturers scourge him, false witnesses lie about him, soldiers mock and spit on him, the crowd jeers at him, and even God seems to abandon him. Who would want closeness with a God who "wills" such pain?

Jesus, The Dying-Resurrected One

The following questions are for your prayer as well as your reflection. Take some time right now. Ask God directly:

> What do you, God, "will" for Jesus in Gethsemane?
> What do you want for him, and by extension, for us?
> What do you passionately desire, God?

The Fourth Gospel can correct our emphasis on God's will as pain, suffering and death. According to this community, Jesus loves to do God's will; his food is to do the will of God (Jn 4: 34). Jesus also says in the last supper discourse that to see him is to see the Father (Jn 14: 9). Thus, if we want to know what God wills, we have simply to look at what Jesus wants. As we move chapter by chapter through the events which John has set before us in this gospel, we can see what Jesus wills, wants and passionately desires. Jesus wills and so God wills:

> Our being with Jesus: come and see (ch. 1);
> Water into wine (ch. 2);
> Our rebirth by water and Spirit (ch. 3);
> Our healing from the need to draw our own water and save ourselves (ch. 4);
> Our wholeness (ch. 5);
> Our nourishment (ch. 6);
> Fountains of living water springing up from deep within us (ch. 7);
> Truth and freedom (ch. 8);
> That we might see (ch. 9);
> Life in abundance (ch. 10);
> Life now and resurrection later (ch. 11).

These are just a few desires of God's heart. This passionate desire of God for us, embodied in Jesus' hopes and desires for us, is Jesus' food and drink. Jesus enfleshes what God wants. No wonder Jesus was so hungry for all that God desires for us

(Jn 4: 34). To see Jesus throughout his ministry spend his time and energy fighting against betrayal, abandonment, physical pain, untruth, abuse of power and alienation from God is to see God at war against those same forms of oppression.

How could God then "will" such an injustice as Jesus' crucifixion? Can injustice make up for sin? On the contrary, as the prophet Jeremiah announced in God's name, "My plans for you are plans of peace, not disaster" (Jer 29: 11). When God suffers with Jesus in the garden of Gethsemane, suffers over the injustice that human beings with free will are inflicting on Jesus, God wills that Jesus too be free. God wills that Jesus be true to himself and faithful to his mission to proclaim the good news of God's unconditional and steady love. Rather than betray all those tax collectors and sinners who had just begun to trust God's love, Jesus would not recant and retire to his carpenter's shop in Nazareth. He was tempted like us in all things, tempted to walk away from danger, pain and death, but instead he trusted that God's plans for his ultimate peace would prevail.

One With Jesus' Dying and Rising

God's action in Jesus' death and resurrection is not for our contemplation alone. Faith, attachment to and commitment to Jesus, also means participating with Jesus in dying and rising. That implies much more than the gift of personal salvation. The experience of being crucified and therefore enlivened through our union with Christ frees us for discipleship, mission and ministry. It orients us to act on behalf of others. Our contemplation of God's action, our prayer, is meant to open us for actual and ever deepening participation in the paschal mystery. First, we participate in Jesus' death through the daily dying involved in human relationships and work situations. Then, we participate in Jesus' resurrection through the daily rising of our hearts in joy, peace, love and gratitude.

The Christian community has tried to express its delight and gratitude and wonder through telling the story of Jesus' death and resurrection in the gospel, and through celebrating the presence of Jesus in the Eucharist. The Eucharist, the community's most profound prayer, re-presents the dying and rising of Jesus. In every eucharistic celebration we proclaim the mystery of faith: Christ has died, Christ is risen, Christ will come again.

We are not meant to be mere spectators in the Eucharist, however. Because through baptism we are plunged into the dying and rising of Christ, because we no longer live but Christ lives in us (Gal 2: 20), we find his dying and rising continuing in our daily lives. Just as Jesus had to die daily, facing disappointment, physical aches, misunderstanding, fatigue, anger, fear, conflict and temptation, so we die many times a day to selfishness and sin. When we experience affection, success, beauty, union, joy — all the various blessings which crowd the day of the one who has eyes to see — we experience resurrection. By paying attention each day to the dying and rising of Jesus continued in our simple, sometimes humdrum living, we can share more deeply in Jesus' own dying and rising. We can offer our dying and rising in the Eucharist.

Baptism is our participation in the dying and rising of Christ. Eucharist remembers, celebrates, invites us to share his death and resurrection. The whole New Testament is centered on this experience: a stumbling block, a foolishness for some; a joy, a hope for others.

John's Gospel carries the same message. *The* sign of God among us is Jesus in the flesh, but a flesh "lifted up" onto the cross and into glory. All the signs Jesus performs point to the ultimate sign of his death and resurrection.

His first sign at Cana manifests his glory and leads his disciples to belief (Jn 2: 11). Although his signs show Jesus' dependence on his Father (3: 2), they are meant to lead us to see and to believe (6: 30) in him. According to John, believing in Jesus is more than intellectual assent to truth, more even than acknowledgment that he is the Christ, the Son of God (20: 30–31). Believing means union with Jesus, and that is eternal life (6: 47). All the signs lead to life.

The final part of John's Gospel contains the last supper discourse. That long speech ends with Jesus' prayer that God's name be glorified and that we may share in the glory-filled union of Father and Son. Unlike the synoptic evangelists, John does not picture an agony in Gethsemane but instead has Jesus meet and direct his captors with a cool and calm majesty. Instead of elaborating bloody tortures, John focuses on a dialogue with Pilate about truth and authority. Instead of an inscription, Pilate writes a title for Jesus' cross that proclaims him king. Even though these are small details, John is describing Jesus as freely laying down his life for his friends, mounting the cross like a throne. Always in command, Jesus arranges for his mother's welfare. Then, without any loud cry of abandonment as in Mark, the king on the cross announces, "It is accomplished" (Jn 19: 30).

In John, Jesus' final act is his giving the Spirit. The Spirit could not be given until Jesus was glorified (7: 39). According to John, Jesus is actually glorified on the cross. His resurrection and ascension and "handing over" the Spirit are simultaneous with his death in John's theology. His being lifted up is an exaltation. "If I am lifted out of (literally) the earth, I will draw all to myself' (12: 32).

The Book of Glory concludes like the synoptic gospels, with stories of the empty tomb and appearances of the risen Lord. The glory that has shone through the words and work of Jesus is now available to empower us, his disciples. The Book of Glory becomes a promise of our own future glory.

Guided Prayer Passages

1 Corinthians 1: 22-25; 2: 1-5

> Jews ask for signs and Greeks seek wisdom, but we proclaim Christ crucified, a stumbling block to Jews and foolishness to Gentiles. To those who are being called, however, both Jews and Greeks, Christ is the power of God and the wisdom of God. The foolishness of God is wiser than the wisdom of human beings and the weakness of God is stronger than that of humans....

Look for a while at a crucifix. Is this foolishness? Is it weakness? How do you feel? Is it difficult to think of Jesus crucified? Why? Why not? Are you angry? Afraid? Depressed? Grateful? Wondering? There are no wrong ways to feel, or no emotions which are holier than others. Talk over these feelings with Jesus. Read the passage again and respond.

2 Corinthians 4: 7-11

> We have this treasure in earthenware vessels so that the marvelous power might be acknowledged as God's and not ours. We have been afflicted in every way but we are not held down, in difficulties but not despairing, persecuted but not abandoned, cast down but not dead. We are always carrying the dying of Jesus in our bodies so that the life of Jesus might be apparent in these same bodies. We are always being handed over to death because of Jesus so that the life of Jesus may be revealed in this mortal flesh of ours.

How are the things you suffer similar to Jesus' agony? Can you remember specific times in your past when life and resurrection joy have sprung from those very difficulties? Ask for the power of the resurrection to become apparent in your life today.

Romans 6: 3–4

> Do you not know that all of us who have been baptized into Christ Jesus were baptized into his death? We were buried with him by baptism into death so that as Christ was raised from the dead through the glory of the Father we too might walk in newness of life.

In baptism, we are immersed in the dying of Christ, plunged into his pain. Sometimes that suffering is only too real in our individual lives. Sometimes the pain of the world, our families and friends, arouses our compassion, our own ability to suffer with others.

Perhaps at your baptism water was poured over your head. Image yourself now as an adult plunging into the ocean, a lake or river. Feel what it is like to be totally immersed in the living water who is Christ. Image every drop of the ocean as the other human persons around the world and through the ages who have been plunged into Christ. Ask for the gift of compassion to know, to feel and in some small way to act in solidarity with all who live or have lived in Christ.

Romans 8: 28–32

> We know that for those who love God, those called according to God's purpose, everything works together for the good. God first knew us and wanted us and conformed us to the image of the Son, so that he should be the firstborn among many brothers and sisters. And those whom God first knew, God called and justified. Those whom God thus made holy, God also glorified. What shall we say about all this? If God is for us, who could be against us? If God did not spare the Son but gave him to us all, how much more God wants to lavish on us all that God is!

God will not fail to lavish on us all that God has to give! We might expect God to give us all we *need,* but to give us all that God has to give? We might expect God to mete out, but to *lavish* on us? God wants to lavish. What in you blocks God's lavishing on you? Ask for the grace to receive all that God wants to give.

Romans 8: 33-39

> Who will bring a charge against the chosen ones of God? If God sets us right, who can condemn us? Could Christ Jesus? He did indeed die, but was raised from the dead and is at the right hand of God, making intercession for us. Who will separate us from the love of Christ? Could affliction or distress or persecution or famine or nakedness or danger or sword? ... No, we have overcome all these things through Christ who loves us. I have become certain that nothing, neither death nor life nor angels nor rulers; neither things present nor things to come; neither powers nor height nor depth; nothing in all creation will ever be able to separate us from the love of God in Christ Jesus, our Lord.

Paul believes and trusts completely in God's love made available in Christ. We can learn from his belief, tried and found true by our saints throughout the ages, that nothing, not even mortal sin, will make God stop loving us. We have the free will to cut ourselves off from God, but even then God goes on loving us. How do you feel about that? Tell God. Perhaps you will have to argue it out together. Perhaps your belief matches Paul's. Respond as you feel inspired.

1 Corinthians 15: 42-44, 51-56

> Regarding resurrection from the dead. What is sown is corruptible and it is raised incorruptible. What is sown in dishonor is raised in glory. What is sown in weakness is

raised in power. What is sown as a natural body is raised as a spiritual body....

Look! I tell you a mystery. We will not all fall asleep, but we all will be changed in a moment, in the blink of an eye, at the last trumpet. For a trumpet will sound and the dead will be raised, incorruptible, and we shall be changed. What is corruptible will put on incorruptibility, and what is mortal will put on immortality. Then shall this word come to pass: "Death is swallowed up in victory. Oh death, where is your victory? Oh death, where is your sting?" Now the sting of death is sin, and the power of sin is the Law. But thanks be to God who gives us the victory in Christ Jesus, our Lord.

Here is the Christian hope against our society's pervasive "denial of death." Whether we are dead or still living at the "last trumpet," we shall all be transformed. With your baptism, the resurrection has already begun in you. Tell the Spirit in what concrete ways you want to be transformed now, today. "Thanks be to God who gives us the victory through Jesus Christ." Remember areas of sin in your past life that have been healed, and then change Paul's line to "Thanks be to you, God," composing a personal litany of gratitude.

Galatians 2: 19–21

Through the law I died to the law so that I might live toward God. With Christ I have been co-crucified. It is no longer I who live, but Christ lives in me. The life I now live in the flesh, I live by faith in the Son of God, who loves me and gives himself for me. I will not push aside the grace of God, for if holiness were possible through keeping the law, then Christ died for no reason.

Paul says he has been put to death with Christ on the cross. If you have been baptized, you have also shared this experience.

Look at a crucifix. You began this book hoping to grow closer to God and Jesus. How close do you want to be to Jesus? Really? Share your feelings with him.

Galatians 2: 19–21 (above)

"It is no longer I who live but Christ lives in me." Discipleship for Paul does not mean carrying our cross alone, but rather, discipleship is a profound union with Jesus. It is letting Jesus continue his dying and rising in us. Paul does not suggest, as the synoptic gospels do, that we externally follow and imitate Jesus in his life and death. Rather, our discipleship is interior. Gradually Christ takes over our lives and lives through us. Talk with Jesus about this kind of discipleship.

2 Corinthians 4: 10

We bear in our bodies the dying of Jesus so that the life of Jesus might be apparent in these mortal bodies of ours.

Ask that Christ might be seen today by all who see you. Pray John Henry Newman's prayer: "Let them look up and see no longer me, but only Jesus."

John 11: 33–44

When Jesus saw Mary (of Bethany) weeping and the Jews who were with her weeping as well, Jesus groaned in his spirit and was troubled. He said, "Where have you put him?" They said to him, "Come and see." Then Jesus shed tears. Some Jews said, "See how he loved him...." Jesus, again groaning within himself, came to the tomb. It was a cave, and a stone was lying before it. Jesus said, "Take away the stone." Martha, the sister of the one who had died, said to him, "Lord, by now he smells, for he has been dead four days...." Jesus cried with a loud voice, "Lazarus, come out." The dead man came out, bound hand and feet with winding cloths, and his face bound round in a napkin. Jesus said to them, "Untie him and let him go free."

Where do you want healing in your life? Where do you need new life? Tell Jesus as you watch him stand in pain, in tears before the tomb. He calls out for new life: "Lazarus, come out.... Be fully alive."
Now hear him call your name: "_____, come forth.... Be fully alive." Ask Jesus for the ability to receive love and freedom from others and from him, to allow others to free you of some of your bonds. In what do you find joy? What makes you glad to be alive? Life, your "aliveness" is a gift. With whom is Jesus asking you to share your life now?

Faith-sharing

When your small group gathers for faith-sharing, use the above scripture passages which you have prayed over as the basis for your sharing. Refer to the suggestions in the Invitation if needed.

Small Group Exercises

1. Can your group remember the five sorrowful mysteries of the rosary? Can the group remember the fourteen stations of the cross? When was the last time anyone heard a sermon on the suffering and death of Jesus? In your family/community/ parish, which is the greater celebration: Christmas, Easter or Good Friday?
Was it a new idea for anyone that the Eucharist is a celebration of and participation in the dying and rising of Jesus? If it was not

a new idea, can you remember when and where you heard it? Besides fear of powerlessness, denial of death, denial of sin, or the false fear of "God's will," why does our first world society shy away from the cross? Or does it?

2. Let each one in the group ask ten people, Christian or non-Christian, how long they think the world (this planet earth) will survive, and what will be its cause of destruction? Do any of those interviewed suggest the Second Coming of Christ to establish the reign of God? If you propose that idea to them, what is their response? If they reply that they don't know, ask whether their basic response to Christ's return is fear or joy. Share your results in your group.

3. If your group got a special message from God that Christ would return one year from this day, how would each of you personally feel? What would you do? If you would make any group response, what would/could you do? Be sure to allow time for reflection before answering.

Concluding Prayer

To remember, according to Jewish spirituality, is to make present. Take some time to make present through memory, first Jesus, and then those family and friends who are now resurrected with Christ. We begin with a reading about the collective suffering of all God's people.

Leader:
> A reading from the Suffering Servant Songs of Isaiah (52, 53): My servant will be lifted up, exalted. Once we were ashamed to look at him, a being no longer human. Kings stood speechless before him. Without beauty, without majesty, he is despised and rejected by all, a man of sorrows, familiar with pain. He bore our sufferings, carried our sorrows; he was pierced for our offenses, crushed for our sins. Through

his pain he offers us peace; by his wounds we are healed. His anguish over now, he has seen the light.

After some silent meditation, the leader may light a Christ-candle or other candle as a sign of resurrection. Take five minutes of silence to address each of your own deceased loved ones by name, remembering them as vividly as possible. Then let each group member call out the names of his or her dead-and-risen loved ones.

After each person's list, let the group respond, in gratitude for their mortal and immortal life, with the psalm verse used by the early Church to celebrate the resurrection (Psalm 16: 9, 11):

Together:

Their heart exults, their body again rejoices.... You lead them on the path to life, abundant joy in your presence forever.

5

Jesus, the Disciple and Apostle of God

Questions

- How have you described a disciple of Christ? Have you made a distinction between an apostle and a disciple? If so which word better fits you, or at least your desire?
- How could Jesus be known as a disciple by his earliest followers? How is Jesus an apostle?

Scriptural Message

Paul

Paul was so identified with Christ that he could claim, "It is no longer I who live but Christ who lives in me" (Gal 2: 20). Paul knew himself to be a disciple, a learner from Christ and his Spirit. As the disciples of rabbis learned by imitating their master, so Paul imitates Christ, and more: Paul "puts on" the Lord Jesus. And he urges his followers to do the same, "Be imitators of me, as I am of Christ" (1 Cor 11: 1).

Paul identified with Jesus the disciple, and also with Jesus the apostle, the one sent by God, who called Paul to be "an apostle of Jesus Christ" (2 Cor 1: 1). As we have seen, Paul's passionate thirst was for a life-long learning of the mysteries which he stewarded. He was both disciple and apostle.

John

Although Paul's own spirituality is apostolic, it is John's Gospel which portrays Jesus with an apostolic spirituality. In John, Jesus is both a disciple of God and the apostle of God.

As a disciple, Jesus learns from God. "No one has ever seen God, but the one who is closest to the Father's heart, he has made God known" (Jn 1: 18). The one who abides in the Father's heart, learning from God, is then sent *(apostolos)* to make God known, and is thus also an apostle. (The Greek word for "make known" is *exegesato* from which we derive our word exegesis, the art of drawing the meaning from a scripture text.) In a very real way, Jesus draws out for us the meaning of God who is the source of scripture, the source of all life. Jesus exegetes the Father. Jesus is sent not only to lay open the Father before us, but to invite us just as close to God's heart as he is. *"As* you, Father, are in me and *as* I am in you, may they be in us" (17: 21). "As" here means "in the same way, with the same depth, the same intimacy."

Jesus does not merely reflect the Father. Because of their mutual living in each other, because of the unity between them, because of their mutual knowing which is really loving union, Jesus' mission and ministry embodies all that God has longed to say and do for people over the centuries. God who kept sending both word and Spirit to Israel finally sent Word in human flesh and Spirit in our flesh to reveal the very heart and mind of God.

Throughout John's Gospel we hear and see just how close Jesus was/is to God's own heart. They share one and the same life (5: 26). Jesus has put flesh on the grace and truth, the unconditional love and fidelity, the *hesed* and *'emet* that characterize God. If we want to know what God is like, what God wants, we look at what Jesus is like, what Jesus wants.

To see Jesus in action is to see God in action. Jesus can do nothing except what he sees his Father doing (5: 19). To hear Jesus speak is to hear God speak: "What I heard from him, I speak in the world" (8: 26). He does nothing, says nothing but what he has learned from God (8: 28). He describes himself as "a person who has spoken the truth to you which I heard from God" (8: 40).

Jesus' body and emotions, his healings and foot washing, his laying down his life for his friends, not only express God but embody God, all God's hopes and tenderness and anger and joy. The events of Jesus' life, according to John, are signs of God's love and service of us. In each of Jesus' experiences, the Word continued to become more and more flesh, God continued to be more and more bodied forth into the world, grace and truth continued to be more and more available to us in Jesus, who is the sacrament of God.

Because God is mystery, Jesus continues to know and love and learn from his union with God. Jesus continues as God's disciple and, as God's apostle, is sent day by day to bring us good news, life in abundance.

Guided Prayer Passages

John 14: 9

Whoever sees me sees the Father.

More than merely imitating God, Jesus lets God speak and work through his body, his life and his love. And he commissions us to be sacraments of himself to the world. *"As* the Father sent me, so I send you" (20: 21), Jesus says, and not just to the people gathered in the upper room on Easter night. Jesus sends us, too, to enflesh God. When, in the past week, did God speak or work through your body, your life or your love? When were you a sacrament of Christ, an attractive sign of God, to your family, colleagues, neighbors, parish, community?

John 1: 35, 37–39

> The next day John was standing with two of his disciples.... Two disciples followed Jesus. Jesus turned, saw them following and said to them: "What are you looking for?" They said to him: "Rabbi (which is translated Teacher), where are you staying?" He said to them: "Come and you will see."

If those two disciples were braver they might have asked, "Who are you?" Take some time alone now to ask Jesus "Who are you? Where do you live and work today?" Listen. Then read his words as directed to you, for they actually are: "What are you looking for?" What do you want? Tell him.

Faith-sharing

When your small group gathers for faith-sharing, use the above scripture passages which you have prayed over as the basis for your sharing. Refer to the suggestions in the Invitation if needed.

Small Group Exercises

1. Jesus is hungry to do the will of God. If we want to know the will of God, we only need to look at what Jesus wants, what Jesus passionately desires. Using your memories of all four gospels, reflect on what you see Jesus wanting. After some moments of silent remembering, share your reflections. Then discuss how the sentence: "It must be the will of God" has become such a hollow, "non-response" to people who are suffering tragedy. Share what each group member does or says when tragedy strikes a friend.

2. What has Jesus come to do? What has he taught us about God? Why did God send him? What is the good news he proclaimed? Discuss. Each member will probably have more than one way to respond to those questions. "Out of his fullness we have all received, grace upon grace upon grace" or, as it were, "life, life, life!" "I have come that you may have life," not in trickles, not in fits and starts, not just on sunny days, but "life in abundance!" This is one possible response to the above questions. Take five minutes of silence, alone but together. When in your life have you felt fully alive, "all systems go," felt life in abundance? Let your memory dwell on the scene, the event, the person who sparked that abundance. Feel that life in abundance. Then share the memory and your feelings with your group.

Concluding Prayer

Leader:

Let us listen to Jesus speak these words directly to us:

The Lord God has given me the tongue of a teacher and skill to console the weary with a word in the morning. The Lord God sharpened my hearing that I might listen like one who is taught. (Isaiah 50: 4)

In silent prayer, we ask Jesus to teach us personally, to open each of us to learn (discipleship) what God wants us to do on behalf of those who need God's love and service embodied in us. We ask ourselves where we might be sent (apostleship). Allow some silent time to let the Spirit teach you.

Leader:

Individually, let us now express out loud how the Spirit is moving each of us. (Allow time for each group member to speak if he or she wishes.)

After each has spoken, is there any consensus in the group about any local area of need? For example: the handicapped of your parish, the shut-ins of your neighborhood, the homeless of your city, and so on.

Is there just one group of people that sparks your attention, for whom all of you can in some small way "lay down your life?" If you can come to consensus on one group of needy people, then simply keep your eyes and ears open to the truth of their situation all week. See how your new alertness makes you tune in differently to TV, newspapers, anecdotes at work, etc. Ask co-workers, friends, relatives what they know about this situation, where you might find more information.

After time for the above discussion, pray the following words of Jesus together.

Leader:

We conclude with Jesus' commission, spoken directly to each of us personally, and to our group:

Together:

Peace be with you! As the Father has sent me, so I send you ... Receive the Holy Spirit. (Jn 20: 21–22)

6

Jesus, the Bread of Life

Questions

- How important is bread in your life? How important is it in our culture, in other cultures?
- As you see starving people and refugees, shown frequently on the nightly news, how do you feel? What do you want for them?

Scriptural Message

Paul

Although Paul did not refer to Jesus as the Bread of Life, he did understand Christ to be our nourishment. All of us are one loaf, and that is Christ. "The bread that we break, is it not a communion in the body of Christ?" he asks his community at Corinth (1 Cor 10: 16). He answers his own question in the next verse, "Because there is one bread, we although many are one body, for we all share the same loaf."

The bread of life is real food, and a prophetic call to decision. Let each one examine whether he or she eats "the bread of the Lord" with a discerning faith, Paul insists. "For as often as you eat this bread and drink this cup, you announce the death of the Lord, until he comes" (1 Cor 11: 26–28).

John

It is a well-tested truth: one cannot give what one has not received. Jesus, then, can only give us the bread of life if he himself has been nourished. God feeds him. His food, Jesus tells us in John's Gospel, is his Father's will (4: 34).

Throughout chapter six of this gospel, often called the "bread of life discourse," the Father of Jesus is central. There are many motifs that John wants to weave through this long discourse, but Jesus keeps centering back to the Father. This man whom they want to make king is a man who knows how to receive from God. He receives the light of God's glory and now *is* the light of the world (8: 12); he receives his own food and drink through union with God (4: 34) and so becomes and now *is* bread for the world.

People of Jesus' time believed that when the Messiah came, God would renew the gift of manna, bread from heaven. And so, Jesus proclaims: "I am the bread of life." John's Gospel shows just how much more Jesus can offer. He is the true bread which nourishes more than physical hungers.

The Torah, the rabbis were teaching, was true food for the spirit, likening the law to manna. "The law came through Moses," John comments in 1: 17, but life, grace and truth come through Jesus, who gives us a new word of spirit and life (6: 63) and a new bread which is his very self (6: 35).

The law, Torah, was the word and will of God for the Jews, a sign of their covenant union with God. For Christians, the word and will of God is now embodied in the flesh and blood of Jesus. Instead of being brought into union with God as the Jews are, through profound union with God's self-expression in the law, we are to eat Jesus' flesh and drink his blood for an interior, profound union with God in and through the Son.

"As the living Father sent me and I live because of the Father, so the one who eats me will live because of me" (6: 57). The Johannine key word "as" opens up infinite possibility for us. Jesus lives because of his Father; Jesus receives everything from God;

Jesus is totally identified with his Father; Jesus is rooted in God, embodying God, closest to the Father's heart. That is just exactly what is meant to happen to us when we eat Jesus: we live, we receive all that Jesus is, we become thoroughly identified with him, rooted in him, embodying him, closest to his heart. Baptism begins the process of identification with Christ, but eating the bread of life strengthens that baptismal identification.

This is God's will: that the giver of life himself becomes the bread of life, our bread. The Word of God becomes totally flesh in the very act of dying, of surrendering his flesh and blood. This flesh given in death is "life for the world" (6: 51). This is Jesus' passing over from life to death to new life. This is the Christian Passover, identified as we are with him, flesh of his flesh and blood of his blood. God wills that we have eternal life, both now and when Jesus raises us on the last day (6: 38–40).

In our first-world society, it is hard for us really to feel physical hunger or thirst. Food, drink and so much else is abundantly available to us. That is why it is good to juxtapose passages that tradition has applied to Eucharist, and specifically to communion, with passages on Jesus' food: the will of God. Frequent reception of communion only makes us holy if, being so identified with Jesus in baptism and in Eucharist, we find our true food in God's will.

Eucharist calls for commitment to God's will and commitment to each other. Eucharist challenges us to *be* what we eat, the body and blood of Christ in our world. The body and blood of Christ is not a thing, an object. The body and blood of Christ is a living person, Christ offering himself in teaching (3: 1–15), welcoming the outcast (4: 7–42), healing (4: 46–5: 9), feeding the hungry (6: 5–13), confronting for the sake of justice (7 and 8), helping others see (9: 1–41), leading (10: 1–18), giving life (11: 17–44), serving (13: 3–15), praying (17: 1–26), laying down his life freely for his friends (18 and 19), drawing all into one new and true family of God (11: 51–52).

All of these specific ways (and many more) of laying down our lives on behalf of others are the challenge of our baptismal identification with Christ. The bread of life gives us the courage, energy and strength to respond to that challenge. More, it gives us Christ himself deep within us to continue his work, taking flesh day by day in us. Our hunger and thirst may be either grossly or subtly self-centered in our rich and willful society. But they are meant to turn us outward to others through our eating Jesus' given-over flesh and drinking his poured-out blood.

Guided Prayer Passages

John 6: 11–15, 25–29, 32–37, 41, 43–45, 53-56, 60, 66–68

> Jesus took the loaves, and having given thanks *(eucharisto),* he distributed to those reclining, both the loaves and fish, as much as they wanted. When they were filled, he told his disciples, "Gather the leftover fragments, so that nothing may be lost."
>
> So they gathered and filled twelve baskets with the fragments from the five barley loaves, the leftovers after everyone had eaten. When the people saw the sign he did, they said: "Truly, this is the prophet coming into the world." Jesus, knowing that they were about to come and seize him in order to make him king, left for the mountain by himself....When the people found Jesus ... he said to them, "Truly, truly, I say to you, you are seeking me not because you saw signs but because you ate the loaves and were satisfied. Do not work for perishable food but for living food, living on to life eternal, which the Son of Man will give you. This one God has sealed."
>
> They said to him, "What should we do that we may do the works of God?" Jesus answered them and said, "This is the work of God: that you believe in the one whom God sent.... It was not Moses who gave you bread from heaven, but my Father gives you the true bread from heaven. The true bread

is that which comes down from heaven and gives life to the world." They then said to him, "Lord, give us this bread always." Jesus said to them, "I am the bread of life. The one who comes to me shall not hunger and the one who believes in me will never thirst. But I told you that you have seen me and yet you do not believe. All that the Father gives me will come to me and the one coming to me I will never cast out...."

The Jews then murmured about him.... Jesus responded: "Do not grumble among yourselves. No one can come to me unless the Father who sent me draw that person, and I will raise such a person up on the last day. It is written in the prophets: 'They will all be taught by God.' Everyone who has heard and learned from the Father comes to me....

I am the bread of life.... If anyone eats this bread, that one will live forever. The bread which I will give is my flesh for the life of the world.... Unless you eat the flesh of the Son of Man and drink his blood you do not have life within you ... for my flesh is food indeed and my blood is drink indeed. Whoever eats my flesh and drinks my blood lives in me and I live in that person."

Many of his disciples, hearing this, said, "This is a difficult word. Who can hear it?" After that many of his disciples went away and walked with him no longer. Jesus then said to the twelve, "Do you also want to leave?" Simon Peter answered him, "Lord, to whom should we go? You have the words of eternal life."

Try to visualize these various scenes in your imagination as if you were there. What do you smell, what is the weather like, what are you wearing, what is Jesus wearing, how does the bread taste, what are your feelings? How do your feelings change as you get involved with Jesus in this scene? Maybe Jesus offers some asides, comments just to you, or maybe you'd like to ask him a question or ask him to repeat a line. Get your whole self — mind, heart, emotions, senses, memories, desires — into this episode. It is a difficult and convoluted chapter but the more graphic your imagination, the more sense it should make to you.

John 6 (above)

Theologian Gustavo Gutierrez notes that there are two reasons for first-world Christians to choose to be poor, for as he and we know, poverty is not a positive value in itself. He writes that the value of poverty for us (and we add: the value of hunger for us), lies in our being somewhat able to identify with the poor (and the hungry), and in our being counter-cultural. Ask the Spirit to sharpen your hunger for justice and for the inclusion of all in the distribution of the world's goods. Then ask for the courage to be even a bit counter-cultural. This week, ask the Spirit to show you someone you may be afraid of, look down on, or even despise. Just state your fears or prejudices to God/Jesus/ Spirit and let the Paraclete begin to convince you otherwise (Jn 16: 8–11).

John 6 (above)

Jesus offers himself in so many ways. In which of those ways has Jesus offered himself to you? In what other concrete, specific ways has he given himself to you? Which of the gifts and services mentioned most fit your talents and desires? In other words, of all the ways mentioned, which ones are you already embodying? Which ones do you want to embody? Share your desires, your hungers with him.

John 6 (above)

When millions today are starving for lack of bread, Jesus claims to be bread for the world, bread of more profound, real and everlasting nourishment. Let us use our bodies to symbolize and through imagination feel-with and pray on behalf of those who are so desperately hungry.

Close your eyes, clench your teeth, make fists and try to feel pain in your empty stomach for a few minutes. Then pray: "God, with your starving people, I am angry, hurt, and feeling betrayed by the world and even by you. Please let your Spirit show me my own hurt and hungry places as I try to rest in you." The Lord speaks: "If only you would open your mouths, how I long to feed you. I would feed you with the finest wheat and honey from the rock" (Ps 81).

Now, with open eyes, mouths and hands, pray: "Lord Jesus, open our mouths and feed us with the real food of yourself."

Faith-sharing

When your small group gathers for faith-sharing, use the above scripture passages which you have prayed over as the basis for your sharing. Refer to the suggestions in the Invitation if needed.

Small Group Exercises

1. Luke the evangelist twice states that Jesus grew in grace. What does that mean? Johannine scholar C. H. Dodd says the Word became totally flesh in his dying. Do you believe that? Karl Rahner sees the incarnation, not as occurring in a split second in Mary's womb, but as a lifelong process, the process of Jesus' becoming more and more human, a process climaxing in his death. What does it mean to grow in grace? And what relation does that have to becoming fully human?
2. How can we not only *give,* but *be* bread for the world?

Concluding Prayer

A litany of thanks for God's will, God's passionate desire, as found in each chapter of John's Gospel.

Leader:

> For your will, your desire to be with us —
> All respond after each phrase:
> Thank you, our God.

Leader:

> For your will, your desire to make the water of our lives a rich wine ...
>
> For your will, your desire that we be born into the new life of the Spirit ...
>
> For your will, your desire to heal us from the need to save ourselves ...
>
> For your will, your desire to make us whole ...
>
> For your will, your desire to feed us ...
>
> For your will, your desire to fill us with fountains of living water ...
>
> For your will, your desire to teach us truth and set us free ...
>
> For your will, your desire to open our eyes to your love and service ...
>
> For your will, your desire to lavish on us life in abundance...
>
> For your will, your desire to raise us up now and on the last day ...

Leader:

> Let us pray together for God's will to be done on earth as it is in heaven.

All recite together:

> Our Father, who art in heaven, hallowed be thy name ...
> Amen.

Leader:

> May you bless us, Jesus, and pour into us your great desire, your hunger and thirst to do the will of the One who sends us, now, in your name.
>
> All: Amen!

7

The Human Situation: Grace and Sin

Questions

As we begin, reflect on your personal experience of grace. Instead of constructing a definition of grace to use, remember certain events, persons, desires, insights, choices, etc. ... which were "grace" for you.

- What did these various experiences have in common?
- What has happened to you because of grace?
- What did sin mean to you as a child? As a teenager? What does it mean to you now?
- How did your experience of sin change?
- What are the current situations in which you find yourself limited, weak? How do you feel when you discover a new physical, spiritual, or relational limit?

Scriptural Message

Paul

Grace to Be Loved Sinners

Only if we actually experience grace can we truly know our sinfulness. When Paul was overwhelmed by grace on the road to Damascus, he recognized his perfection and self-satisfaction as so much garbage. Not only did Paul think he was sinless as he hurried north along that road, he thought he was perfect in keeping the law. But when, in a flash, he came to know Jesus, he could see for the first time just how sinful and self-serving his religiously exact life had been. He had been busy saving himself. To Paul, salvation was his project, not God's.

Then Christ took hold of him (Phil 3: 12). As Paul was brought more intensely into the mystery of Christ year after year, he began to recognize his sinfulness and neediness. With this new vision, he could call his perfectionistic law-keeping and his spiritual credentials garbage (Phil 3: 4–14). When he knew how dearly he was loved by Christ he could let down his defenses, his self-won perfection. He could admit who he truly was in Christ: a weak, needy sinner incredibly loved just as he was. He was touched by grace long before he could ever lift a finger to earn it. As he phrases it, he was loved and chosen before he was even born (Gal 1: 15).

Many of us think of grace as *a thing,* a free gift of God, perhaps even God's own life. Grace, however, is not so much a thing as *a Person.* Grace is not a static gift but a dynamic process. Grace is not God's life packaged and given, but God's very action of giving God's own life and love to us. God pours out unconditional, extravagant love, and that pouring out is grace. And when God wants to lavish love on us, it is freely lavished, not as a reward for any work or good deed. Grace cannot be earned.

God's unconditional love helps us be free: free to admit who we are, to admit our weaknesses, our rebellion, our self-complacency, our hate and prejudice and manipulations. God does not ask us to change or demand us to "shape up" before loving us. God just keeps pouring love into us, even if we make ourselves God's enemies (Rom 5: 5, 10). Nothing can separate us from the love of God. Gradually, only God's love frees us, transforms us (2 Cor 3: 17–18).

Yet we can refuse to be loved so extravagantly. We can blush and say we're not worth it, we're no good, we're so sinful. We can scrape our consciences and obsessively take our spiritual pulse. We can squelch the movements of the Spirit within us, all in the name of growing in perfection. Soul-scraping, however, is not a true acknowledgment of our sinfulness but a self-centeredness that poses as humility. Instead of keeping our eyes fixed on Jesus, such scrupulosity (if it is not a mental illness) keeps our eyes glued firmly on ourselves. At times, we may need to be converted from wallowing in this kind of false guilt. Instead of being converted from sin, some of us, like Paul, need to be converted from our "goodness," from our attempt to create our holiness as we think it should be.

On the other hand, having a true sense of creaturehood and of our sinfulness and guilt is God's gift to us. Knowing our sin, we can rejoice in our smallness or boast of our weakness, as Paul put it. When we are weak then God's power is strong to save (2 Cor 12: 9–10). Where sin abounds, the pouring out of God's own self (grace) more abounds (Rom 5: 20). When great saints confessed their sinfulness, they were not pretending. The nearer they were led to God's own holiness, the more their sinfulness became clear to them. In all their weakness they clung to Jesus, rather than to their own goodness or to their ideal of perfection.

Not only did Paul experience himself personally saved, but he knew that the world, even sinful Greco-Roman society, was reconciled to God through Christ. In Christ, God's offer of personal and social reconciliation was made available for all those who would accept it. Paul expressed some of the wonder of this reconciliation when he wrote, "In Christ there is no Jew nor Greek, no slave nor free person, no male nor female but all are one in Christ Jesus" (Gal 3: 28). The barriers between human beings are broken, and reconciliation is effected. Social sin has been conquered. Racism and nationalism (Jew/Gentile), classism (slave/free), sexism (male/female) have been healed in Christ Jesus. Even the created universe, nature itself, is reconciled and graced (Rom 8: 22–23).

Yet we still find so much that needs healing and change in our modern society. Even graced as we are, knowing ourselves to be delivered from sin, we find ourselves caught in the evils of racism, classism, sexism.... How to understand these seeming contradictions?

The way Paul understands this ambiguity in our lives is the "already/not yet" dynamic. The universe is already reconciled, and not yet. We are already dead to sin, and not yet. We have all been raised with Christ, and not yet. It seems that many of us can resonate with that in our own life experience. Already/not yet. Succinctly then, and paradoxically, we are graced sinners.

The experience of being graced "promotes us to sinners," as Jesuit theologian Brian McDermott explains Sebastian Moore's phrase. When we know how loved and saved and grasped and claimed we are, we can dare to be what we are in all truth: loved, graced sinners. That was Paul's experience. What we may judge as Paul's arrogance is actually his knowing without a doubt that he was special to God, not because he was holy, zealous, or loving, but because as sinner he was in Christ Jesus, and thus saved.

Paul had various ways to describe sin and its effects. He termed it disobedience to God. He pointed out our sinful tendencies and our unredeemed areas of living and loving, our all too natural inclinations which Paul called "flesh" *(sarx* in the original Greek). Paul also writes about more serious sin, what we today would call mortal sin. Writing to the Galatians, he insists that there is indeed one way to be cut off completely from Christ: "You are severed from Christ, you who would be justified by the law. You have fallen away from grace" (Gal 5: 4).

Why is Paul so adamant that we not try to save ourselves by keeping the law? Why is he so enthusiastic about our freedom from this law? His insistence seems to flow from his own personal experience of being saved and freed. If we use the law of God to justify ourselves, thinking that through the law we can achieve salvation or holiness, then Christ died in vain, he writes. What meaning did that terrible crucifixion have if we could somehow be certain that we are right with God? On the contrary, we can never be sure, because certainty negates faith. We live not in certainty but in ambiguity, always having to trust that Jesus' death and resurrection has righted (the meaning of "justification") our relationship with God. Only Jesus saves. Only he continues to free us.

In the obedience of Jesus, all humankind was at last obedient to God. In Jesus' receiving from his Father all that God wanted to lavish on him — God's own self — all of us were opened to God's self-giving. It is in Jesus that we are saved and graced, not by accomplishing good deeds, although these flow from our joy and gratitude for being so well loved. Faith means union with Jesus. It is by this union that we are justified and that we have peace with God (Rom 5: 1).

We cannot measure, we cannot claim, we cannot be certain. In the midst of ambiguity about our sin and our freedom, we can only trust and cling and respond as best we can to such an extravagant outpouring of God's love and life, in Christ Jesus.

John

The Light of Life

Let us consider the symbol of light in John's Gospel. John frames sin and grace in symbols of darkness and light. Our knowing God, our learning truth, our seeing the glory of God shining out of Jesus, and Jesus himself in glory lighting up every creature from within — all these are centered in the symbol of light. "His life is the light of us all," John's community proclaims (1: 4). His life is grace upon grace upon grace upon grace, and out of his fullness we have all received (1: 15–16). Light is the symbol of grace and "the darkness was not able to overcome it" (1: 5). Christ is himself light.

Light shining in the dark places of our hearts is John's way of imaging Paul's sin and grace dynamic. For Paul sin lurks in *sarx* (flesh). This does not mean the flesh of our human bodies or our sexuality, such splendid gifts of God to us. Paul understands flesh as the bits of our self which we keep hidden and try futilely to control, the areas of darkness which we refuse to let Christ touch. For John, on the other hand, flesh is positive. The *sarx* of the Word made flesh heals our *sarx* and sin. The Word made *sarx* lights up the dark and secret places in our hearts.

In John's Gospel, the story of the man born blind is a prominent symbol of one who comes into the light of life (ch. 9). This healed man is in crisis because he has met the Light, Jesus. Crisis *(krisis* in Greek) means judgment, a time for decision. How shall the healed man now see and make a true judgment? For what will he decide: the light of Jesus or the dark of legalism as its own end? For whom will he decide?

When Jesus gives light we, too, are called to judgment, crisis. John's Gospel calls us to choose boldly: either light or darkness. And while we do have this basic option, this gospel also acknowledges how gradual the action of light can be, penetrating, healing and transforming dark places in our hearts and in our world. For example, in John's third chapter, Nicodemus comes to learn from Jesus at night; in chapter seven, he is more bold, and in Jesus' burial scene, he is fully "in the light," helping with Jesus' body.

According to John, sin is disbelief, our refusing to hear the word of God through and in Jesus. To refuse to see Jesus is another way in which John portrays sin (9: 41). The word which Jesus speaks will be our judge on the last day (12: 48), but the light who is Jesus causes us to judge ourselves in the here and now. Both in John's understanding of *krisis,* and in Paul's understanding of "now is the acceptable time," judgment is today.

Jesus announces: "For judgment I came into this world, that the ones not seeing may see and the ones seeing may become blind" (9: 39). Yet Jesus claims not to judge. What John is saying is that *krisis is* a self-judgment. Each time we see the truth of our life in the light of Jesus we either choose to remain in the light and actually embrace the light, or we choose blindness, darkness. And even when we are in the light, day-to-day decisions still call for a choice to allow a deeper penetration of that light into our hearts, and through us, into our society.

Jesus is sent not to condemn but to save. He is the sign, the *krisis* (3: 19), the decision-point. Those who do evil hide away so as not to be exposed by the light, but "the one who does the truth comes to the light so that the works done in God may be shown forth" (3: 21). The phrase "comes to the light," is in the present tense, continuing day by day. It is the light who is Christ that fills us with grace and thus reveals our sin.

Again there is no need to rub our consciences raw looking for sin. We need to respond to the gentle light which beckons us to look at our sinful places and to choose truth over self-deception. The light of Christ transforms us from within, gradually lighting up the dark places in our hearts that we hide even from ourselves. We can welcome this light as it comes to us from reading scripture, from the word of a friend, a movie, a very special or a very ordinary event. So much of creation, so many people can be sacraments of light for us.

In this light of Christ, we can see ourselves as God sees us and begin to love ourselves as unconditionally as God loves us. We can love even the dark crevices of our hearts with the sure hope that eventually, when we are ready, the light will shine in them, will heal and transform them. "His life is the light of us all" (1: 4). Through our daily choosing the light which Jesus offers, through our union with his transforming light/self, our life as individuals and as Church becomes light.

A Johannine morality might be characterized as living more and more deeply in an ever-growing light. A Pauline morality might be characterized as living and responding to God's love and God's people ever more freely. In viewing sin, both authors would urge us to move away from a taboo-style morality in which we, like animals, cringe in fear when we have done something wrong. Such guilt is far from adult contrition, and prevents a mature, trusting admission of sinfulness. Nor need we awkwardly force some harsh moral code upon ourselves, for by doing so, we would still be trying to save ourselves rather than trusting in God. Instead, both John and Paul would urge us to respond to God's first having loved us. It is God's love which makes us moral, and indeed, holy. "Perfect love casts out fear (1 Jn 4: 18), and only God's love is perfect. It is not that we have first loved God, but God has first loved us (1 Jn 4: 19) and is constantly lavishing on us all that God is (Rom 8: 32).

Guided Prayer Passages

Isaiah 60: 1-3, 19–20

> Arise! Rise clothed in light. Your light has come and the glory of the Lord shines on you. The nations shall march toward your light and their leaders to your sunrise. You will no longer need the sun by day nor the moon by night. The Lord shall be your everlasting light; your God shall be your glory. Your sun will never set and the days of your sadness shall be ended.

After reading the above passage aloud, sit for three or four minutes in silence and total darkness. Ask to remember a time of darkness or confusion in your life. Try to be specific in your memory, recalling concrete details and especially your feelings during that time.

Then light a candle and try to read the Isaiah passage in the dim and flickering light, which symbolizes the ambiguity so familiar to us, which calls us to trust only God. Finally, turn on all the lights in the room and read the passage, for the third time in the clear light of Christ. You might even sing it, making up your own tune. Share your feelings with the risen Lord who shines in your darkness.

You might try this three-fold reading with all the following passages, asking to accept the ambiguities and paradoxes of our faith, and asking to feel and know the light within.

Romans 5: 6-11

> While we were yet weak, in the proper time, Christ died for the unholy ones. Even for a good person, hardly anyone will dare to die, but what highlights the love of God for us is that while we were yet sinners Christ died for us. Now that we have been set right with God, justified by his blood, how much more will we be saved by him from the wrath which is to come. For if while we were enemies we were reconciled to God through the death of God's son, how much more we will be saved by the life of God's son! And so we rejoice in God through our Lord Jesus Christ through whom we have received reconciliation.

Here Paul uses the imagery of sacrifice, which later generations of Christians would associate with pain and death. Jews, however, understood the blood of sacrifice to symbolize life being offered to God. Jesus lay down his life rather than recant one iota of the good news. Ask for the grace of really believing this and rejoicing in it. Because Paul knew he was loved this much — even when he was a sinner — he was fearless in proclaiming this good news.

Notice the progression. First Paul writes that we were powerless to do good. True, but God loves to help the weak. More, we were sinners. True, but Jesus came to call sinners. More yet, we were even God's enemies. True, and yet God still and completely loved us, even and especially because we were running away from such unconditional love. How does this make you feel? Express those emotions to God and Jesus.

Galatians 2: 15–3: 2

> We who are Jews by birth, not sinners from among the Gentiles, know that a person is not justified, set right with God because of works of the law. Not by keeping the law but by

> believing in Jesus Christ are we justified. By works of the law no one is set right with God....
>
> Through the law I died to law that I might begin to live for God. I have been crucified with Christ. So I live, no longer I, but Christ lives in me. In my flesh I live by faith in the Son of God, who has loved me and given himself up for me. I never want the grace of God to be set aside. If, however, we can be justified by keeping the law, then Christ died for nothing.
>
> Oh foolish Galatians! ... Did you receive the Spirit because you kept the law, or because you believed the good news?

How have you come to receive the Spirit? Why does God love you? Ask God directly. Does God love you because you keep the commandments, or because you love and follow Jesus, or simply because God is good, unconditionally and faithfully loving? Ask God what makes you so pleasing, so special.

Galatians 3: 24–27

> The law was our guardian, our trainer, preparing us for Christ, that we might be justified by faith. Now that faith has come, we no longer need that guardian, the law. Through faith you are all children of God in Christ Jesus. All of you who were baptized, plunged into Christ, have put on Christ.

For Paul, the law was like a tutor. But Jesus calls us to make decisions based on him, to learn day by day how to cling to him (for that is what Paul means by "faith"). Our adult moral response as Christians is not based on law, but is a response to a person, Christ, who continually calls us to love. What is more satisfying to you — a set code which you rely on to establish your security with God, or a growing relationship with God's Son which gives you another kind of security? Be honest as you discuss this with the Lord.

Romans 8: 19–20

> Creation has been tied up in futility, not willingly, but because God made it subject in hope. Creation will itself then be set free from the slavery of decay to enjoy the freedom of the glory of God's children. We know that the whole of creation groans together in labor pains together until now.

Read these verses aloud three times. Then take a walk and look deeply at nature, enjoying the beauty and responding to it. Later watch the TV news and see in what ways we human beings have frustrated nature, shackled it. Try to feel the tension in nature itself — both the beauty and the terror. If you decide to bring your observations to your group, be concrete as you describe the beauty and freedom of your nature walk. Be specific as you describe the distortion of nature which you witnessed on the news.

2 Corinthians 5: 18–21

> This is the work of God: God has reconciled us through Christ and has given us the ministry of reconciliation. God was in Christ, reconciling the world to God's own self, not attributing their trespasses to them, and placing in us the word of this reconciliation. Thus we are ambassadors for Christ, with God begging through us, and we beg for the sake of Christ: Be reconciled to God! For our sake, God made the one who did not know sin to be sin in order that we might become, in Christ, the very holiness of God.

Only if we know how much we lack peace and unity in our hearts, our families, our country, can we appreciate what being reconciled means. Ask Jesus to show you where in your own heart or in your relationships you need reconciliation. Then read the passage again and respond to him with your feelings and desires. Ask Christ to make you his ambassador of reconciliation, to plant his word of peace in you, and to make you grow gradually into the very holiness of God, making you an attractive sign of that holiness to the world.

Galatians 3: 28

> In Christ there is no Jew nor Gentile, no slave nor free person, no male nor female.

Ask the Spirit to call to your mind a time when you felt discriminated against. Was it because you were a woman or a Catholic or a certain nationality or certain economic class? Remember the incident as vividly as possible: see the people involved, hear them, feel again your emotions at the time. Then stop. Watch Jesus walk into the situation. What does he do, say? To you, to the other(s)? When he has finished his work in this situation of discrimination, how do you respond to him? Pray, asking him to remove social injustice: racism, classism, sexism, nationalism from you and from communities around the world.

2 Corinthians 12: 7–10

> To keep me from being puffed up by pride, I was given a thorn in the flesh. Three times I prayed to the Lord about this, asking to have it taken away. Christ's answer was: "My grace is enough for you. My power is most strong when you are weak." So I am happy to boast of my weakness in order to experience Christ's power. I can be content with weakness, insults, hardships, persecution, difficulties for Christ's sake. For when I am weak, then I am really strong.

When have you seen Christ's power at work in your limitations, weakness, frustration, hardships, in your being misunderstood or persecuted? Ask the Spirit to show you. After looking at your life with Jesus, narrow it down to just this week's setbacks. Ask him to be strong in your weakness. Savor the concrete memories of God's care and ask for deeper trust in God's saving power.

John 3: 14–16, 19

> As Moses lifted up the serpent in the wilderness, so must the Son of Man be lifted up that whoever believes in him may have eternal life. For God so loved the world that God gave the Son to the world ... not to condemn the world, but that the world might be saved through him.... The light has come into the world.

More glorious than the bronze serpent which Moses lifted up in the wilderness (Num 21: 6–9), Jesus is lifted up as the healing sign of God so loving the world. He is raised as a beacon of light so that, by choosing light, we may have eternal life now. Choose the light, choose healing right now, and tell Jesus your unequivocal choice. Then let him respond to you.

John 1: 4

> His life is the light of us all.

Recall a moment of light in your life, a discovery, an insight. Try to be as specific as possible, asking the Spirit to help you remember. What feelings did you have then? What feelings arise now as you relive the experience? Share your experience and your feelings with Jesus, the light of your life.

Faith-sharing

When your small group gathers for faith-sharing, use the above scripture passages which you have prayed over as the basis for your sharing. Refer to the suggestions in the Invitation if needed.

Small Group Exercises

1. How can your group bring light to the darkness in our culture? How can the laser Light of Christ dispel the social sin around us? If the group is ready to take some small action, discuss how you will do this. Be very concrete. Here are three examples, ranging from the very simple to a more complex and complete commitment:

Phoning local, state or national government

Who precisely is willing to phone or email about a certain issue, to protest or to thank your representative? What is the deadline? What are the necessary email addresses or phone numbers you will need?

Visiting those in need in your neighborhood or parish

Who precisely will visit the homes of the homebound or neglected of your parish? How will you ascertain their individual needs and respond to them? Let those who feel shy about such visits role-play some possible conversations.

Organizing a tutoring program for a nearby jail or prison

Who precisely among you will contact the chaplain to find out the needs of the prisoners? Discuss the talents in the group that might be shared with prisoners: teaching of math, creative writing, watercolors, typing, macramé, etc. ... Who will go, how will you travel? When? How long is your commitment? Tutoring is only one possibility. Not everyone needs to tutor; even writing letters to prisoners is a service. Whatever you decide, it may well provoke a *krisis* in your group. That is the nature of decisions. Try to be specific in planning this Light-bearing: Who will do what? When? Where? How? For how long? After answering all these practical questions, take a few moments of silence and then answer this question: Why are you choosing to reach out? Share your response aloud.

2. Singing is a wonderful way of expressing faith. Make a group list of twenty or so favorite hymns. Do they celebrate grace or sin? What do you learn about the working of grace through their lyrics?
3. Novels, movies, plays, artwork and popular songs can be experiences of grace. Have each group member prepare to explain how a certain novel, movie, etc., sparked a moment of grace in your life, and perhaps taught you about God's self-giving or about sin.
4. Like the wheat and the weeds in Jesus' parable (Mt 12:24–30), sin and grace exist side by side, not only in the world, but in us. Jesus says we are not to judge, but to allow God to separate the weeds from the wheat. When we die, we trust God to judge us kindly. Take a week to find symbols of this ambiguity in nature (for example, shadows of clouds across the full moon), in world events, in your own family/community/parish life. Share these with your group. If you include examples from your personal life, be sure you don't share more than you are comfortable revealing.

5. What have you been taught about sin? What have you learned about sin by reflecting on God, Jesus, your own experience? Is John's understanding of sin too vague for you? What concrete examples of "walking in darkness" or "hiding from truth" do you find in society, in the Church, in your own life?
6. How would John instruct us to examine our consciences? How would Paul? Which is more meaningful to you, and why?
7. Let three different readers proclaim these three selections from the gospel:

John 8: 12

> Jesus spoke to them, saying: I am the light of the world. The one who follows me will in no way walk in darkness, but will have the light of life.

John 11: 9–10

> Jesus answered: Are there not twelve hours in the day? If anyone walks in the day, that person does not stumble because he or she sees the light of this world. But if anyone walks in the night and stumbles, it is because the light is not in that person.

John 12: 35–36

> Jesus said to them: For a little while the light is still with you. Walk while you have light, lest the darkness overtake you. The one who walks in darkness does not know the way. While you have the light, believe in the light that you may become the children of light.

Allow some silence in which you ask the Light to teach you the truth needed for salvation. Then, let the group freely comment on the meaning, the concrete application of the verses to each one's daily living and loving. Build on comments of one another, but remember to discuss, not argue. Because the evangelist John's symbols have many meanings, as many ways of lighting up our daily life as there are people, each personal application of a verse is correct.

Concluding Prayer

The leader needs a flashlight to pray from Psalm 27. Darken the room and light just one candle. All pray together as an antiphon Psalm 36: 9:

Response:

> In your light we are bathed in light.

Leader:

> Let us remember and rejoice that

Together:

> In your light ...

Leader:

> The Lord is my light and my salvation. Whom should I fear? Why should I be confused?

Together:

> In your light ...

Leader:

> One thing I ask of the Lord, this I really want: To make my home in the house of the Lord all the days of my life.

Together:

> In your light ...

Leader:

> I want to gaze on the beauty of the Lord. "Come!" my heart cries, "Seek God's face."

Together:

> In your light ...

Leader:

> I *will* seek your face, Oh Lord, for you are my light and my love.

Together:

> In your light ...

Part Three

The Spirit of Christ and Our Response to God's Transforming Spirit

The Spirit: The Active Presence of Christ

We have heard, seen, felt, known the goodness of our God in Jesus. We have felt God's desire to replace our sin with a lavishing of grace. Now, we open ourselves to God's coming close in the Spirit.

Both Paul and John highlight God's gift of the Holy Spirit. In fact, Holy Spirit, God's life and love poured into our hearts, is another name for grace. Through the Spirit, God lives within us. Just as in one period of history, God came close through the humanity of Jesus, Paul teaches that in our day, the Spirit is Jesus' way of being with us. Not only is the Spirit poured out, but the Spirit acts, transforming us from glory to glory. According to Paul, the Spirit bonds us together and gifts us as the Body of Christ. John uses a variety of images for the Spirit of Jesus. The Fourth Gospel also focuses on the actions of the Spirit and names the Holy Spirit "the Paraclete."

To study and learn from the Spirit is to worship. And our worship calls us to action, truly to be the Body of Christ in our world today, in loving union with Christ and one another. Being the Body of Christ, enlivened by the life blood of the Spirit, brought into loving union with Christ and one another, is exactly what makes us Church.

8

The Spirit: The Active Presence of Christ

Questions

- What has been your personal devotion to the Spirit over the years: as a child? A teenager? An adult?
- What has your church's devotion been like?
- Remember some concrete times in your life that you know were Spirit-filled. How did you know they were full of the Spirit?

Scriptural Message

Paul

God's Love Poured Out

In attending to the Holy Spirit, we begin with the letters of Paul. Paul grounds the whole of Christian spirituality itself in the Spirit who first loved us. The Spirit is God's love poured into our hearts (Rom 5: 5), equipping us to respond to God in a Spirit-ual life. Because he is a Jewish theologian, Paul usually pays attention to how God acts, how Jesus operates, and how the Spirit functions rather than offering and explaining philosophical definitions of their beings. His theology of the Spirit is not concerned with the *being* of the Spirit, which would fascinate later Greek theologians. Rather Paul focuses on the *doing,* the work of the Spirit.

Later generations of theologians will distinguish three persons in a triune God. But Paul, while usually opening and closing his letters with an acknowledgment of the Father, the Lord Jesus Christ, and the Holy Spirit, does not distinguish so much between them. In fact, he actually identifies the Spirit with the risen Lord: "Now the Lord is the Spirit. Where the Spirit of the Lord is, there is freedom" (2 Cor 3: 17).

Paul experiences the risen Lord as present and active, but not in form and feature, like a vision or an apparition. Rather, Paul experiences Christ Jesus in the outpouring of the Spirit. In other words, the Spirit is the way the risen Christ lives with, communicates with, moves, bonds, and loves the community. The Spirit is the risen Lord's way of existing in the world and in human beings. The Spirit is God's transforming power: "Where the Spirit of the Lord is, there is freedom ... we behold the glory of the Lord. What is more, we are being transformed into the same image, from glory to glory. Such is the influence of the Lord who is Spirit" (2 Cor 3: 17–18).

For Paul, the major work of the Spirit is multifaceted. Some of the Spirit's functions are: the transforming of the world and the human heart; the bonding of God's people with God, Christ and each other; the freeing of people from slavery to sin, law and death; the gifting of Christians with love, peace, joy and all the fruits of the Holy Spirit, as well as with gifts for mission and ministry.

Uniting Us and Transforming Us

Having been converted from his self-centered grasping at perfection, Paul is God-centered and experiences the Spirit of the risen Lord as an expression of God's love. This love poured out is not a once-for-all event but a continual rush of love. The Spirit continually keeps Paul united with *Abba*, the word we are given as Jesus' familiar name for his Father (Gal 4: 6; Rom 8: 15). (In fact only in these two Pauline passages, and once in Mark 14: 36, is this intimate Aramaic form of "father" used in the New Testament.)

Never does Paul take it upon himself to cry *Abba*. In both Paul's references, *Abba* is "cried" by the Spirit of Jesus. It is a passionate call to God as dearest parent. It is the Spirit's cry, a prayer from deep within where the Spirit also intercedes, pleading for us "with sighs too deep for words" (Rom 8: 26). It is a constant plea, a "praying always" for which we can take no credit. It is an unutterable desire for union with God which is itself that union. This union is the work of the Spirit, nothing that we could ever earn or deserve.

To be so close to God means to be aware of God's holiness and, by contrast, to be keenly aware of our sinfulness. As Paul teaches from his own experience, if our bodies are dead in sin, our spirits are alive in the Spirit (Rom 8: 9–11). The Spirit is continually transforming the *sarx* of us, the flesh, those sinful inclinations that we hide away from the redeeming light and love of Christ.

Freeing Us from Sin, Law, Death

Not only is the Spirit continually at work bonding us with God and each other and transforming us, but the Spirit is also continually setting us free from sin and death, for "such is the influence of the Lord who is Spirit" (2 Cor 3: 18). (Influence literally means a flowing into, a word which characterizes the gentle power, the *dunamis,* of our lavishing God.)

"Where the Spirit of the Lord is, there is freedom" (2 Cor 3: 17). The personal freedom with which Jesus of Nazareth acted has become available in the unleashing of the Spirit into the lives of all Christians through baptism and in the Eucharist (1 Cor 12: 13). Baptism and the Eucharist are sources of the Spirit and of freedom from sin, law and death.

Those of us baptized as infants, however, may not have reflected on and claimed for our own all that freedom in the Spirit can mean. The Pharisee Saul, as a young rabbinic student, was brought up in the law of God but became obsessive in its observance. Perhaps we, too, know a certain slavery to law. After his conversion, Paul writes that he became more tempted to sin because the law told him that certain actions were wrong. He realized only too well how perverse and conflictual the sin/law dynamic was. The constant pull almost drove him wild, and yet, how could he escape? Even after his conversion, Paul's cry was one of desperation: "Who will save us from this body of death?" (Rom 7: 25).

Gradually, God changed his cry of anguish to *Abba,* the cry of the Spirit of freedom. Yes, Paul writes, Christians are free to do anything. He adds, however, that he will not let just anything "make free with him." That is, by the power of the Spirit, he will not be enslaved by anything again (1 Cor 6: 12). Freedom in the Spirit does not lead to license to do anything at all, but to a nonlegalistic way of relating with God. For example, if our bodies are temples of the Spirit then we can hardly abuse them with excesses of food, drink, or sex (1 Cor 6: 14–20). Instead of avoiding such sin only because the law commands it or even because of the natural outcome of excess, we reverence our body as the home of the Spirit who continually cries *Abba* from deep within. Instead of a fearful focus on sin, we can enjoy a peaceful focus on the Spirit in action.

But if we really are free, why is our struggle with temptation so strong? Part of the answer lies in the already/not yet approach to the human condition. Even more, perhaps we have not yet experienced the Spirit's freeing power in our lives because we never have made a personal choice, an adult decision to claim the power of our baptism. We may not yet have made a conscious choice to be buried to sin in Christ Jesus and to be made alive to God.

Perhaps we are afraid of freedom; maybe we still need to measure ourselves by the law to be certain that we are right with God. Perhaps we have not yet matured to a point where we even want God's freedom, so strongly encoded in our nerve cells are the childhood warnings of our parents (even if they are long dead), the expectations of others, the conventions of society. Who can save us from this kind of death? The Spirit has already begun, Paul assures us. "The law of the Spirit is life" (Rom 8: 2).

Gifting Us for Others

Christian life is a life for others. The Spirit gifts us with union and freedom for the sake of others. Paul could write, in his overstating, passionate way, that if only the Jews could accept Christ, he would be willing to be cut off from Christ forever (Rom 9: 3). He would lay down his life, his life in Christ which was the only life that really counted for him, on behalf of his brothers and sisters.

Love, joy and power are often associated with the Spirit in Paul's writings. The outcome of the Spirit's lavishing is a loving life, an attractive witness of joy, a radiant power even when we seem weak. There is a law, Paul writes, which does not enslave us but serves to open us to others. "Bear one another's burdens and so you will fulfill the law of Christ" (Gal 6: 2). Where do we get the energy to bear burdens?

The word "energy" in Greek is *dunamis*. This word also means power, a term which Paul associates with the Holy Spirit. Just as the Spirit bonds us with God, so the Spirit is that creative energy and power that unites us with each other. The energy expresses itself in the fruits of the Spirit, given to us for the sake of others. Paul calls us to walk in the Spirit, to be led by the Spirit. Then the fruits of the Spirit's activity deep within us will gradually become apparent in our living for others.

How do we know if our life is for others, if our decisions are of the Spirit? If we cannot rely solely on the law to guide our decisions and actions, then where can we put our trust? Paul answers that we can trust in the Spirit who is fruitful.

In making decisions, we can begin with sweeping questions. Does this decision move us toward death or life? Toward slavery or freedom? Toward self-centeredness or other-centeredness? We know we are living in the Spirit if our decisions lead us to gradual growth toward life and freedom and others.

When we need to decide between two goods, however, the question may be more subtle. Which choice will best foster our growth in the fruits of the Spirit, "love, joy, peace, patience, kindness, goodness, faithfulness, gentleness and self control" (Gal 5: 22–23)? Note that fruits are not virtues that we practice. Who can "practice" joy? Fruits are the Spirit's work. We can provide only the soil, the dirt. God gives the sun, the water, all that we need to allow the Spirit's fruits to grow.

Fruits and gifts of the Spirit are given to us not just for our own life and freedom, but for the sake of others. Those others are intimately and forever joined with us by the bonds of the Spirit in the Body of Christ. Whether the Spirit's gift is union, freedom, energy or those fruits that Paul lists in his letter to the Galatians, all these are given us for the building up of the body of Christ.

Guided Prayer Passages

Romans 8: 14–18

> All who are led by the Spirit of God are children of God. For you did not receive a spirit of slavery tying you up again in fear. You have received the spirit of adoption. Thus we cry, through this Spirit: *Abba*, Father. The Spirit bears witness to our spirit that we are indeed the children of God. If we are children, then we are also heirs, heirs of God as well as joint-heirs with Christ. Since we suffer with Christ, we will also be glorified with him.

The Spirit links us continually with God, crying: "*Abba*, Father!" The Spirit prays constantly within us, even when we are not conscious of the Spirit's action. In your imagination right now move through your day and thank the Spirit for praying within you while you showered, drove to work, read your e-mail, checked the TV guide, played with your children. The Spirit prayed deep within you even while you slept. Like all of our spiritual life, so also prayer and union with God are God's work, nothing which we can achieve (Eph 2: 8). Ask the Spirit to be able to trust that good news, to trust the Spirit's prayer deep within you.

Romans 8: 26–39

> The Spirit takes a share in our weakness as well. When we do not know how to pray, the Spirit begs on our behalf with unutterable groanings. And the One who searches hearts knows the mind of the Spirit, because the Spirit is interceding for us according to the desire of God. We know that for those who love God all things work together for the good. We are called according to God's purpose. God has always known us and has always wanted us made in the image of God's own Son, so that he might be the firstborn of many brothers and sisters. And those whom God always knew, God called. God's call means that God has justified us and if justified, then God glorifies us as well.
>
> What can we say? If God is for us, who can be against us? If indeed God did not spare the Son but handed him over for our sake, how much more God will lavish on us all that God is!
>
> Who will bring a charge against the chosen ones of God? God is the one who justifies us and sets us right. So who can condemn? Christ Jesus, who having died is now raised to the right hand of God, also begs on our behalf. Who will separate us from this love of Christ? Affliction, distress, persecution, famine, nakedness, peril or sword? ... I am certain that neither death nor life, neither angels nor rulers, neither things present nor things in the future, neither powers nor height nor depth nor any creature at all will ever be able to separate us from the love of God in Christ Jesus our Lord!

Because it is the Spirit praying, we will never have a bad prayer period. Our feelings may not be all "juiced up," but all things work together for those who love God. Ask the Spirit to open you up to believe what Paul has written here, to the realization that you are lovable and lavished upon by God. Then return to the verses above that are good news for you. Savor them.

Romans 8: 15–16

> You did not receive a spirit of slavery, tying you up again in fear. You have received the Spirit of adoption. Thus you cry, through the Spirit: *Abba*, Father.

Spend ten minutes or so letting the Spirit cry *Abba* deep within you. You might begin with a centering prayer, speaking the word *Abba* yourself until you feel the power of the Spirit taking over. Or you may simply listen, waiting to hear the Spirit's prayer in the silence of your own body and mind.

Not all of us call God *Abba*. If you cannot hear this name for God, ask the Spirit to let you listen to what name of God the Spirit cries deep within you.

Philippians 1: 4–11

> I thank my God at all times when I remember you. You are in every prayer of mine, and every petition on your behalf brings me joy. I am so grateful for your partnership with me in the gospel from the first day until now. I am utterly confident that the One who began this good work in you will bring it to completion on the day of Christ Jesus. It is right for me to feel this way about you all because I carry you in my heart. And you have me in your heart, for you share grace with me, both in my chains and in my defense and confirmation of the gospel.
>
> God is my witness, how I long for you all in the very depths of Christ Jesus. I pray that your love may yet more and more abound in full knowledge and discernment. Then

> you will be able to distinguish and to be sincere and blameless in the day of Christ. May you be filled with the fruit of holiness through Christ Jesus to the glory and praise of God.

For what do you long? For whom do you long? This passage does not mention the Spirit explicitly, but since the Spirit is the love of God poured out in our hearts (Rom 5: 5), bonding us in the depths of Christ Jesus, we can discern Paul's affection and desire as movements of the Spirit of love. Beg the Spirit to bring what God has begun in you and through you to completion. As the Spirit overshadowed Mary and made her fruitful (Lk 1: 35), ask the Spirit to form Jesus in your body, your mind and your will.

2 Corinthians 3: 17–18

> Now the Lord is the Spirit. Where the Spirit of the Lord is, there is freedom. With no veil over our faces, we behold as in a mirror the glory of the Lord. What is more, we are being transformed into the same image, from glory to glory. Such is the influence of the Lord who is Spirit.

How has the Spirit been influencing you through your study of the writings of Paul and John, and through prayer? How has the Spirit been transforming you? How do you feel? Tell the Spirit what more you want. Be bold in your desires.

Galatians 5: 1

> For freedom Christ has set you free. Let no one make you a slave again.

In the past, who or what has enslaved you? Remember in concrete detail a time when you were a slave to someone or something. Discuss with Jesus how you felt during that time. Ask him to show you what things may still hold you captive. Ask him for freedom. How in the past were you set free? Try to be very specific in your memory. How does the memory make you feel? Tell Christ about your memories and feelings. Ask him (not yourself) where he still wants to free you. Ask for the gift of his Spirit.

Galatians 5: 18

> If you are led by the Spirit you are not under the Law.

Ask Jesus to teach you what obedience to the Spirit (not to the law) means.

Romans 8: 19–25

> The sufferings of this present time, I conclude, are not worthy to be compared with the future glory which will be revealed to us. The anxious watching of all creation will be transformed into the eager expectation of our being revealed as children of God. Creation has been tied up in futility, not willingly, but because God made it subject in hope. Creation will itself then be set free from the slavery of decay to enjoy the freedom of the glory of God's children. We know that the whole of creation groans together in labor pains until now. Not only creation, but we ourselves, who have the first fruits of the Spirit, also groan in labor pains, eagerly waiting for our adoption, the setting free of our very bodies. In hope we were saved. But hope that is seen is not hope. For who hopes for what we see? But if we do not see what we hope for, then we eagerly await it in patience.

We often can feel the tension between the beauty of our freedom and the terror that arises from being free and responsible. We are groaning and waiting for full freedom. What are your particular tensions? Discuss them with Jesus. Ask for a deeper awareness of and a fuller participation in the groaning of the Spirit within you.

Romans 8: 26

> The Spirit takes a share in our weakness ...

When has the Spirit come to share in your weakness? Be concrete. Imagine those situations vividly. Feel the Spirit present and working in those situations, both then and now again as you remember.

Galatians 5: 22-23

> The fruit of the Spirit is love, joy, peace, longsuffering, kindness, goodness, faithfulness, meekness and self-control. Over these there is no law.

Use the fruits of the Spirit as a criterion to judge your actions and to make your decisions. Do the decisions you make help you grow in peace, joy, love, kindness ... ? Remember a major decision you made this past year. Ask the Spirit to show you how these fruits have deepened the "rightness" of your decision.

Galatians 5:22-23 (see above)

After some activity today, stop and read Galatians 5: 22-23. What fruits of the Spirit flowed from that activity? How do you feel about that? After some decision you make today, stop and read this same passage. What fruits did you experience after making that decision? How will you respond to the Spirit?

Faith-sharing

When your small group gathers for faith-sharing, use the above scripture passages which you have prayed over as the basis for your sharing. Refer to the suggestions in the Invitation if needed.

Small Group Exercises

1. There are many scriptural names for God. The psalmists had certain names for God. Among other names, Jesus calls God *Abba*. That is the name that Paul heard the Spirit crying in his heart, too (Rom 8: 15). To set the mood, light a candle and open with a spontaneous prayer, asking the Spirit to teach you. Then, slowly and unafraid of silences, call out names for God. You can surely use such biblical names as Shepherd, my Savior, etc. ... But be creative as well: Precious, my Darling, Momma, Grandma — whatever the Spirit cries in you.
2. The Spirit is imaged in scripture as breath, wind, fire, dove. Draw *your* image of the Spirit. Does any musical instrument image the Spirit to you? Any recorded music? If so, bring some music to the group and share this type of Spirit-image. Could you act out the Spirit in some kind of bodily movement? Remember that everyone's image, music, movement is correct, and the variety of images only enriches the group.
3. There is an ancient tradition in the Church, still alive in the Eastern churches and gradually returning in the West, to call the Holy Spirit "She," the feminine face of God. How do you feel about that? What do you think? What difference could this feminine image of the Spirit make in your spiritual life? After some time for personal reflection, discuss.

John

Questions

- When in your life have you had a really good teacher. What made the person so able to teach you?
- When in your life has someone stepped up to defend you when you felt helpless? How did you feel about that person? How did you respond?

🙞 When in some suffering has someone come to comfort you? How were they powerful in this painful situation? What did they do to help?

Scriptural Message

The Paraclete in John's Gospel

John and his community's chief name for the Holy Spirit is Paraclete, sometimes translated as advocate or comforter, who teaches and guides us. Sometimes the Paraclete acts in the same way as the Spirit who was promised in the synoptic gospels, the Spirit given in the Acts of the Apostles and mentioned in Paul's letters. But John's community attributes certain other functions to the Paraclete as well. According to Raymond Brown this leads scholars to conclude that for John the Paraclete is "the personal presence of Jesus in the Christian while Jesus is with the Father." In other words, to experience the Paraclete is to experience the risen Lord. The Paraclete is the radiation, from glory to glory, of Christ. Just as to see Jesus is to see God (Jn 14: 9), so to see the Paraclete at work is to see the risen Lord at work.

We remember that no one has seen God, but the one closest to the Father's heart has made God known (1: 18). None of us has ever seen Jesus in the flesh either, but the Paraclete daily makes Jesus known to us. John's community understands the Paraclete as the disciple of Jesus, because the Paraclete teaches us, just as Jesus, the disciple of his Father, taught his friends. According to this gospel, then, we are disciples of both Jesus and the Paraclete.

Paul teaches that we are baptized into Christ. John's Gospel, however, announces that Jesus baptizes us in the Holy Spirit (1: 33). Baptism in the Holy Spirit is not the prerogative of charismatic Christians. All of us are baptized, plunged into, immersed in the Spirit, on the day of our water baptism.

John uses the water imagery of baptism and focuses on the gift of the Spirit given us in baptism. For this community, we are born anew in the Spirit (3: 5). The Spirit is a fountain of living water welling up within us (4: 14; 7: 37). If, however, the Paraclete is Jesus' way of living within each believer, then John and Paul are proclaiming the same good news: to be immersed in Christ is to be immersed, baptized in the Spirit.

Only in Jesus' last supper discourse does the Fourth Gospel spell out how the Paraclete functions. The Paraclete acts like Jesus, acts in relationship to Jesus, just as Jesus acts in relationship to his Father. Our various translations of the word Paraclete show the depth and range of that action: *advocate, counselor, comforter, intercessor, interpreter.* John also links the Paraclete/Spirit to *peace*.

Jesus promises us "another Paraclete" (14: 16). According to the First Letter of John, Jesus himself is the first advocate (1 Jn 2: 1). We can see Jesus' work continued in the work of the Paraclete. Just as the Father sent Jesus, now both the Father and Jesus send us the Paraclete. Let us examine four more parallels between Jesus and the Paraclete.

First, as human beings one of our primary needs is to belong. On the night before he died, Jesus assures us that we will always belong, we will never be left orphaned. The risen Jesus dwells within us (17: 23). The Paraclete dwells within us (14: 17). We are, whether we feel it or not, totally united with God and with one another.

Secondly, Jesus has made the Father known (1: 18). The Paraclete teaches us, making Jesus known. The Paraclete also brings to our minds all Jesus has taught and is teaching us (14: 26). We are thus in a life-long process of learning, of discipleship.

Thirdly, in the old covenant God's people searched the scriptures, which bore witness to God among us (5: 40). Then Jesus came into the world to bear witness to the truth himself (18: 37). In the new covenant, our times, Jesus' truth sets free (8: 36). It is the Spirit of truth who bears witness (15: 26).

Finally, the Paraclete acts not only as advocate, a lawyer for the defense, but also as a prosecutor of sin. So much of John's Gospel shows Jesus confronting evil, self-deception, error, sin (especially chs. 5, 7, 8, 10). The Paraclete continues to convict the world of sin, to point out error, to show where true righteousness lies, to provoke decision time in our hearts and in society (16: 8–11). In the Fourth Gospel, there is no description of an apocalyptic crisis at the end of the world. Rather, judgment time, *krisis,* is right now. For those who choose life in Jesus now, the Lamb of God takes away all sin (1: 29). Just as Christ removes sin, when the risen Lord breathes the Holy Spirit, the Spirit continues to forgive sin through our own forgiveness of one another (20: 22).

The Paraclete is an image of the Holy Spirit unique to the Fourth Gospel. The priest-poet Gerard Manley Hopkins expands this image in a sermon. Preaching to the British working class, Hopkins deepens our understanding of the word with its nuances of comfort and counsel. From its Greek root (*parakaleo*), Hopkins sees that a paraclete calls forth, calls forward, encourages. He images the Paraclete as a third base coach in cricket, a game like baseball. As we tear around the bases, this Coach waves us home and cheers us on: "Come on, come on, you can do it!"

Besides Paraclete, John gathers other images of the Spirit. Traditionally the dove is an image of the Spirit (1: 32). Images found first in the Jewish scriptures are the wind (3: 8) and the breath of God (20: 22). The Spirit is light in the darkness (16: 8–11), a powerful, effective word (6: 63). The Spirit is the very life of the living bread (6: 63), the very love that bonds us with God, Jesus and one another.

Living Water

A final Johannine image of the Spirit is living water. John envisions the Spirit as a fountain of living water springing up from deep within us (4: 14; 7: 37-39). The key to John's frequent symbol of water is "living." The Jewish people were surrounded by desert and had either to capture rainwater in cisterns or haul well water long distances. For them, fresh and flowing water was such a blessing. God promised through the prophet Isaiah: "You shall draw water with joy from the springs of freedom!" (Is 12: 3–5). To possess living water was a great gift of God. And an even deeper, fresher gift is made possible by Jesus, who quenches thirst with his gift of living water who is the Spirit.

In John's Gospel water conveys different meanings. At Cana, the 180 gallons of water meant for purification in Jewish ritual is transformed into a more joyous symbol: 180 gallons of wine (2: 1–11)! Jesus teaches Nicodemus that we must be born from above, born of water and the Spirit, an allusion to baptism (3: 5). A more subtle allusion to baptism is the man-born-blind's washing in Siloam (9: 7), because Siloam means "The Sent," and we know that Jesus himself is "the One Sent." Water at the sheepgate (5: 2), water to wash his disciples' feet (13: 5), water streaming from Jesus' side (19: 34) are all symbolic of healing, service and an outpoured love.

Two of John's most important references to water indicate that the water which Jesus gives is living, deeply interior, totally satisfying. The first reference is clothed in a powerful story about how Jesus relates with those who are thirsty. It is the story of the Samaritan woman (Jn 4: 7–42). Here, John's community tells of an outcast woman who was thirsting for acceptance, dignity and real love. But this is also the story of a man who was, who still is, thirsting to fill us full.

The second reference is a promise to all of us who desire to come to Jesus. With deep passion, Jesus cries out: "If anyone thirsts, let that person come to me. I will give that person rivers of living water." The community comments, "Now he was speaking of the Spirit who was not yet, because Jesus was not yet glorified" (7: 37–39). When Jesus is glorified, lifted up and exalted on the cross, he hands over the Spirit, the fountain/river of living water gushing from his open heart. He continues his saving action deep within us.

Guided Prayer Passages

John 4: 14

> I will give you fountains of living water.

What is your experience of being thirsty ... for love, security, peace of heart? For what else? For God? Tell God.

John 7: 37–39

> On the last day of the festival, Jesus stood up and cried out: "If anyone is thirsty, let that person come to me and drink. The one who believes in me, as scripture says, rivers of living water will flow from the womb (literally) of such a one." Now he said this about the Spirit which those who believed in him were about to receive. For the Spirit was not yet, because Jesus was not yet glorified.

What blocks you from living life in its abundance? Is there a boulder blocking that river-source, that fountain deep within you, your spring of living water? Speak with Jesus about your resistance. Where is the "water" stagnant in your life? What do you want from the Lord? Tell him.

Amos 5: 21, 24

> I do not delight in your sacred rituals.... Rather let justice roll on like a river, and righteousness like an everflowing stream.

Ask the Spirit to remind you of some specific activity which you once did to further justice, peace or reconciliation in your family, workplace, civic area. Then ask the Spirit to remind you vividly of your feelings as you engaged in the activity. What in your action was like a river of justice, of freedom and peace? Perhaps it wasn't an action rushing like a river, but a trickle of blessing to a warring, greedy world. Trickles can and often do become torrents. What aspect of your outreach challenged you? What aspect made you feel good? Share that with Christ.

John 3: 5–6, 8

> Unless one is born of water and the Holy Spirit, one cannot enter the kingdom of God. That which is born of the flesh is flesh and that which is born of the Spirit is spirit.... The wind blows where it will. You hear the sound but you know neither where it comes from nor where it is going. It is like that with everyone born of the Spirit.

As John's incarnational and sacramental spirituality teaches us, our response to the good news need not be confined to sacred spaces or times set aside for prayer. With images of the Spirit ringing in your heart, go outside and feel the wind. Is there any water flowing near your home? If so watch it, hear it, touch it. If not, find a special bowl, fill it with water and spend some time lifting the water high, watching and listening to it flow back into the bowl. This wind and this water live and move and transform deep within you. What do you *feel?* Share those feelings with Jesus. This *is* prayer.

John 14: 16–18

> I will ask the Father, and God will give you another Paraclete to be with you forever, the Spirit of truth. The world cannot receive the Spirit ... but you know the Spirit, because the Spirit dwells within you and will be in you. I will not leave you orphans. I am coming to you.

Jesus comes to us moment by moment through the Spirit living within us, who keeps us joined to Jesus and to one another. How else has Jesus come to you? In other words, if the Spirit is sometimes called the hidden person of the Trinity, where have you found the Spirit hiding? In what faces, what actions, what services has the Spirit come to you? How will you respond?

John 16: 7–8

> I tell you the truth: it is necessary for you that I go away, for if I do not go away, the Paraclete will not come to you. But if I go, I will send the Paraclete to you. That Coming One will convict the world of sin and righteousness and judgment.

Jesus proclaimed by both word and action that we can be confused about what is good and what is evil. Jesus and the One he left us will straighten out the differences between sin and holiness. According to Jesus' parable of weeds growing among the wheat, we are not to make judgments, not even upon ourselves. This is good news. Here Jesus assures us that we can trust the Spirit to sort out our lives. Turn over to the Comforter now whatever you recognize as your drive toward perfection, the monitoring of your spiritual pulse. Let the Paraclete coach you, counsel you, comfort you. Respond.

John 15: 26–27 and 20: 21–23

> When the Paraclete comes whom I will send you from the Father, the Spirit of truth who proceeds from the Father, that One will witness about me. And you also are witnesses....
> Jesus said to them again: "Peace be with you. As the Father has sent me, so I send you." When he had said this, he breathed on them and said to them: "Receive the Holy Spirit. The sins of whomever you forgive are forgiven and those you hold are held."

Jesus bore witness to God's desire for our peace, both through forgiveness of our sin and through acceptance of our humanity, which is the very flesh that the Word embraced. The Spirit continues Jesus' witnessing to this good news by breathing peace into us, thus enabling us to forgive and to accept ourselves and others. Ask the Spirit to deepen in you this joyful, peaceful experience of God's unconditional and faithful love. Ask the Spirit to equip you as a capable witness to this good news.

Breathe in peace, breathe out a smile. Continue as long as you feel relaxed and receptive.

John 14: 25–26

> I have spoken these things to you while I remain with you. But the Paraclete, the Holy Spirit, whom the Father will send in my name, will teach you all things and remind you of everything which I told you.

Friends teach one another. Who are the best teachers you ever had? What made them good teachers? What did they touch in you? What did you open to them? The Paraclete has been teaching you. What are you most grateful the Spirit has taught you? What do you want the Spirit to teach/touch in you now? ... in your senses? ... heart? ... feelings? ... desires? ... intellect? ...memory? Talk to the Paraclete as your teacher and friend.

Faith-sharing

When your small group gathers for faith-sharing, use the above scripture passages which you have prayed over as the basis for your sharing. Refer to the suggestions in the Invitation if needed.

Small Group Exercises

1. What in this chapter on the Holy Spirit has been a comfort to you? What stretched your ideas and attitudes? What do you think might influence your relationship with the Spirit/Paraclete?
2. Share with your group a past activity which promoted justice, reconciliation or peace (see Amos 5: 21, 24 in the Guided Prayer Passages above). Share the aspect of your outreach which challenged you and the aspect which made you feel good. What do you, personally, want to do next? Is anyone in the group interested in joining you, or are you interested in joining someone else? Perhaps the Spirit will lead some of you to repeat the same activity but this time with a partner or two. Perhaps you will do something different. Discuss.
3. After this discussion, take five minutes to wait in silence as a group for the Spirit's prompting for an activity to promote justice or peace. After the silence, let anyone who is inspired speak. If no inspiration occurs during prayer time, keep alert for a nudge from the Spirit during the day or the week ahead, and bring it to share with the group at your next meeting. Could the group ever agree on one common project?
4. New Testament authors used images for God. What images of the Spirit/Paraclete appeal to you personally? What images can your group brainstorm? Do not limit yourself to biblical or "holy" images (this is the point of sacramental spirituality: all is holy). Remember that in brainstorming there is no right or wrong response. Let your ideas simply flow and see what the creative Spirit teaches you and your group.

Concluding Prayer

Leader:

> Light of lights, in darkness shine.
> Flood our hearts with light divine,
> Burn within us, living Fire!
> What is stained by sin, renew;
> What is dry, with grace bedew;
> Strength to wounded souls restore!
> Coldness with your fire burn;
> Willfulness to wisdom turn;
> Crooked ways make straight once more!
> *(From the Pentecost sequence "Veni Creator Spiritus")*

Response together:

> Lord, send out your Spirit and renew the face of the earth.

Leader:

> Lord, our God, how great you are, wrapped in a robe of light. You make the clouds a chariot and ride on the wings of the wind. You make the winds your messengers.
>
> Response together: Lord, send out ...

Leader:

> You make springs burst out of dry land and grow green things for us, that we might bring bread out of the earth, wine to gladden our hearts, and oil to make our faces shine.
> Response together: Lord, send out ...

Leader:

> The earth is full of your creatures, made by your wisdom, O Lord. All look hopefully to you to give them food at the proper time. When you breathe into them, they live, and you give new life to the earth. (From Psalm 104.)

Response together: Lord, send out ...

Leader:

Where the Spirit of the Lord is, there is freedom. We all reflect as in a mirror the glory of the Lord. We are being transformed into his likeness, from glory to glory. Such is the influence of the Lord who is Spirit (2 Cor 3: 17–18)!

Response together:

Lord, send out ...
Place a large and lovely bowl in the midst of the group. Let each one approach it and "draw deeply from the springs of God's great kindness," as the monks of Weston Priory sing. As a reader prays Psalm 63 in the group's name, let each one scoop up water from deep in the bottom; let it cascade through the fingers. Feel the water.

Reader:

Oh God, you are my God. I seek you early in the day with a heart thirsting for you, a body wasted with longing for you, like a dry and thirsty land, long without water.
With such longing I come before you, to gaze on your power and glory. Your love is better than life. I sing your praise. I bless you all my life. I am satisfied now as at a banquet. I follow you with all my heart.
Then all pray together this Psalm-Prayer:
As deer long for running streams, so we long for you, our God.
With our whole being we thirst for you, our loving God. We praise and thank you for all the ways you make us thirst for you, for justice and peace, for unity. We thank you for fountains of living water which well up within us. Thank you in Jesus' name. Amen.

9

The Church, Ourselves: Sacrament of Jesus and the Spirit

Both Paul and the group originating with John agree that Church means community. Some scholars have claimed that the Fourth Gospel lacks any doctrine regarding the Church. But John's Gospel is birthed and nurtured precisely in the Church, if we consider Church to be not an organizational structure but a community of disciples. Paul not only describes the risen Lord as Spirit, but he also describes his experience of the risen Lord in terms of the "Body of Christ." The Body of Christ, as experience more than image, colors all Paul's further experiences. For Paul the Church is community "in Christ," and indeed is the very Body of Christ alive and active in every age and every place.

Like Paul on the road to Damascus, each of us probably has had an initial, powerful realization of who God/Jesus/Spirit is and what that means for the rest of our lives. We, like Paul, may have to spend a lifetime letting the depth of our initial experience unfold for us.

Questions

- What conversion point, insight, decision or relationship has had an impact on your life?
- What does Church mean to you? How has the meaning changed?
- What does the Body of Christ mean to you? How has the meaning changed? If so, can you pinpoint what caused the change in meaning?
- What has been your experience of community "in Christ"?

Scriptural Message

Paul

The Body of Christ

We begin our investigation of Church with Paul and his experience of community as the Body of Christ. "Who are you, Lord?" Paul asked the Lord. The answer came: "I am Jesus of Nazareth whom you are persecuting." How could that be? Paul knew that Jesus of Nazareth had hung on a tree and died. He was not persecuting the dead Jesus but the followers of Jesus, those who claimed that the cursed one was God's Messiah. Paul had still to learn that God had raised Jesus from the dead and had, through the outpouring of the Spirit, made Jesus live in the hearts of these followers and in the community: "I am Jesus whom you are persecuting in these women and men." Jesus was alive in Damascus. Paul was blind, literally and symbolically.

When Paul met the risen Lord, his whole understanding of God was turned upside down and inside out. God had come close in this carpenter from Nazareth. God had chosen Paul to meet the Messiah both in a revelation on the road, and in his Body in Damascus. God was eager to come close to Paul. And Paul, who had been blind, began to see.

After his baptism, Paul went away to the wilderness of Arabia for three years to ponder this powerful experience in his heart. Paul came to understand that Jesus was extended in space and time (as Pius XII would later proclaim in his encyclical, *Mystici Corporis*). Paul came to understand Jesus as living through the lives of those who believed in him. The identification of Jesus with those who are persecuted resembles Matthew's portrayal of Jesus in need: "When I was hungry, homeless, naked ... whatever you did to the least you did to me" (Mt 25: 31–46). Paul was introduced to a Jesus who was identified with his brothers and sisters. On the road to Damascus, he was introduced to the Body of Christ.

Some scholars hold that the Body of Christ is the most central concept in all of Paul's writings. (The word "body" in Greek is *soma*.) The English bishop and scripture scholar John A.T. Robinson hymns it:

> ... the word *soma* knits together all his [Paul's] great themes.
> It is from the body of sin and death that we are delivered;
> it is through the body of Christ on the cross that we are saved;
> it is into his body the Church that we are incorporated; it is by his body in the Eucharist that this community is sustained;
> it is in our body that its new life has to be manifested; it is to a resurrection of this body to the likeness of his glorious body that we are destined.

We, too, will attend to the many meanings of body: the gift of our own bodies-in-process-of-transformation, the gift of Eucharist, and the gift of community: women and men bonded and gifted by the Spirit to be Jesus in the world today. We pay attention to the "Body of Christ" as the very corporal, tangible way that Jesus' life and whole human person is extended. The Body of Christ is not a metaphor but a mystery, which we shall never finish trying to understand and experience. For Paul, the Body of Christ is no figure of speech, no mere image of reality, but reality itself — quite indescribable, but a reality. Indeed, there may be nothing more real for Paul. He and we are "in Christ," not in some mythical, ethereal, cosmic atmosphere. We *are* the very Body of Christ.

To be in Christ is never a solitary experience but always a being with and for others. "In Christ" is a way of saying that the desperate loneliness of modern humanity is assuaged. What the world needs now is interdependence, especially in the face of such massive pseudo-independence of individuals and nations. That interdependence is accomplished "in Christ." Paul, in his exuberance to describe our interdependence with Christ and with each other, has to coin new words. He writes of followers-together, yokefellows, fellow soldiers, co-workers.

Paul's unique verbs, used nowhere else in the New Testament, sometimes describe our union with Christ, and sometimes our union with one another: *to share with, continue with, suffer with, sent with, planted together, to have the same mind as, to strive together, help together, labor together, groan together, glorified together;* and finally, *"be made into the same form with"* Jesus' death, his glorious body and his image. Paul seems to know that God has myriad ways of uniting us with Christ and with each other.

It is in the body of Christ that we, the baptized, "live and move and have our being" (Acts 17: 8). We "put on" Christ's body, baptized into union with him, "... for you are all one person in Christ Jesus" (Gal 3: 26-28). Many now represent the one. We represent Christ. In Christ, we "who are many are one body for we all share in the one loaf" (1 Cor 10: 17).

> The Body of Christ is:
> the risen and glorified body of Christ;
> the risen body extended in space and time through us;
> the body which we share in the breaking of the bread;
> the body-community which we discern in the eucharistic communion;
> the body gifted with many parts and functions.

There is no Body of Christ in space and time without us, no Eucharist without the offering of the body who is us, no Church which is not us. Christ is not far away sitting on some starry throne; Christ is not a lonely prisoner in the tabernacle. Christ is us, his Body, his whole self extended in time and space to *this* time, to *our* space so that we can communicate him to everyone we meet.

Because we are the Body of Christ, all sin then is against the body. Paul gives us a few examples. To sin against a weaker brother or sister is to sin directly against Christ (1 Cor 8: 12). To join our bodies to the bodies of prostitutes is to take the very "limbs and organs of Christ ... and make them over to a harlot" (1 Cor 6: 15). To eat and drink at communion without discerning a poor member of the community is to eat and drink not Christ at all, but judgment on our lack of love for the Body (1 Cor 11: 27–32).

In other words, if we do not see the Body of Christ in every member of the community, and especially in the poorer or weaker members, and yet we go on receiving communion, we "eat and drink unworthily and are guilty of the body and blood of the Lord" (1 Cor 11: 27). Paul uses very strong language, perhaps strange to us who have often privatized the Eucharist, focusing on Holy Communion and our personal bond with Jesus. For Paul, the presence of Christ is in the community who eats and drinks and remembers. It is in eating the one bread that Christians become one body, the Body of Christ (1 Cor 10: 16). Even if we eat and eat and eat, receive communion after communion, our "communion" will produce nothing more than judgment if we remain isolated, shutting out one or many of the Body.

Grace is found in the Body of Christ. We have died to the law through this Body and are joined to the One raised (Rom 7: 4). Through his Body we have access to God. Grace is found in the Body which is the Church. We, the Church, belong to each other. God makes the ultimate self-gift (grace) through the Body of Christ, who is the risen Lord, living and acting in his members. Note that we are not one Body *in* Christ, a moral or social entity gathered together in Christ. We *are* the Body of Christ (1 Cor 12: 27). We are incorporate in him. (The Latin root of incorporate is *corpus* meaning "body.")

The resurrection of Jesus has both transformed and expanded his human limits and so he is able to welcome us all into himself, to make us his Body. It is the resurrection which makes a real, not metaphorical, identification between Christ and the Church. Later New Testament authors will separate the community from

Christ, naming Christ the head of the Body, or naming the Church the bride of Christ. Not so in Paul's experience. The Church *is* the Body of Christ.

Grace is also located in our own human, sinful, yet in-the-process-of-being-transformed bodies. It is into our bodies that the Spirit is poured, crying *Abba*. We do not belong to ourselves: "... the body is for the Lord ... for you were bought at a great price. Glorify God therefore in your body." Our bodies are God's gift, temples of the Spirit (1 Cor 6: 13–20). Our bodies are sources of grace for each other (1 Cor 7: 14).

Paul understands grace as the gift that, as the fullness of God's own life, brings with it a variety of specific gifts for building up the Body, the Church. Aspects of grace are available to all Christians. For example, union with God and with each other, freedom and its energy, and the fruits of the Spirit belong to us all.

The first of the spiritual gifts is the Spirit's own self, Paul writes, manifested in the heart-cry: Jesus is Lord! And some members of the body have special gifts for special service and ministry. Twice, in Romans 12: 4–9 and in 1 Corinthians 12–13, Paul lists some of these gifts for ministry given by the Spirit for building up the Body of Christ. However, Paul's lists are not exhaustive. He mentions gifts apart from these lists, such as the gift of celibacy. Different generations in the Church's history have named other gifts for ministry, such as exorcism.

In the Corinthian community the gifts of the Holy Spirit were abundant. But Paul learned that the way some members manifested their gifts had become disruptive to the community and a scandal to those interested in joining. Paul had to explain that the Body has its various parts, functions and gifts. Whether a gift was spectacular or an ordinary service, all were necessary for the smooth functioning of the Body. "There are differences of gifts *(charismata),* but the same Spirit. There are differences of ministries, but the same Lord. There are differences of workings, but the same God, the One working all things in all (1 Cor 12: 4–6). After this passage, Paul mentions a variety of gifts, all manifestations of "the same

Spirit." The Spirit is the source both of the Body's unity and of its diversity, gifted by God in their mission and ministry as apostle, prophet, teacher, wonder worker, healer, helper, governor, speaker of tongues. These operate interdependently, as do the various parts of the human body: feet, ears, eyes and so on (12: 14–24). Paul's insistent point is that there is not to be division *(schisma)* in the body, but that the members should "care for one another. If one member suffers, all suffer together; if one member is glorified, all rejoice together" (1 Cor 12: 25–26). "To suffer with" is compassion. "To rejoice with" is Christian love. And of all the gifts, *"the greatest of these is love"* (1 Cor 13: 13).

John

The Church-Community, Sacrament of Life

The Spirit/Paraclete blows freely like the wind, intangible, visible in the fruits by which we can recognize the Spirit, even if only in retrospect. We the Church, the Body of Christ, are *the* sacrament of Christ in today's world. The seven sacraments are signs to *us the members,* who have been drawn to Jesus by God. But the sign that the *world* is meant to see is ourselves as community, in mutual love and unity. We are a new family, a community of disciples; above all, we are the sacrament of Christ.

One Johannine image of the Church is the new family of God. Jesus "died to gather all the scattered children of God into one family" (Jn 11: 52). The sign of life to the world is ourselves, the Church, gathered together because of this death. We belong to God, and are newly constituted children of God, because Jesus has drawn us all together into a new family in his death and exaltation. Lifted up, he shines in the world like a beacon. Sharing his life, we too have become "children of light" (12: 36). Only in John's Gospel does Jesus' mother Mary stand at the cross, a symbol of the new family being generated at that very moment. In giving his mother to the Beloved Disciple, Jesus gives all his disciples to Mary, now our mother in this new family.

The new family of the Church, which begins on Calvary, is effected in the ultimate exaltation on Easter. At the Last Supper, Jesus had called his disciples not servants but the intimate word "friends." After he had risen, the Lord urges Mary of Magdala to tell his brothers and sisters that he is ascending to "my Father and your Father" (20: 17). Here, a new and even more intimate relationship is expressed: the relationship of blood, of family.

Perhaps John's best-known image of the Church is the vine with its branches. Vine and branches are one. We, the branches, utterly dependent on the life-force that flows through the vine, are meant to bear fruit. In John's portrayal of the Church as the vine who is Christ, Jesus issues a warning to those branches that need pruning. And yet, just as he explained his washing their feet, Jesus reassures the disciples and us that we are already clean, already pruned because of the word he has spoken. We are living in his word (8: 31–32) and thus we belong to God (8: 47). We belong and we bear fruit on the vine, source of our life and energy: Christ.

The Johannine community understands itself, the Church, as the community of disciples, sent as Jesus himself was sent. To see this community is to see Christ, who was once and is still light and life for the world. This community is to love one another and has a missionary thrust. The vine is to bear fruit. The new family is to include other "scattered children of God" in the community, whom the Father and Jesus will attract: "No one can come to me unless the Father who sent me draws her or him" (6: 44). Jesus, too, draws all to himself (Jn 12: 32).

How attractive Jesus is in the pages of this gospel. Many of those drawn to him rush away to invite others to come to Jesus as well. John the Baptizer's disciples leave the forerunner to "come and see" Jesus (Jn 1: 37–39). Andrew invites his brother Simon, and Philip brings Nathanael (1: 40–46). Nicodemus at first comes at night (3: 2) but grows bolder (7: 52) until finally he asserts himself before Pilate on Jesus' behalf (19: 39). The Samaritan woman rushes off to invite her townspeople, who then confess Jesus as Savior of the world (4: 42). The man born blind suggests that even the Pharisees might want to become Jesus' disciples (9: 27).

When the Greeks are drawn to him, Jesus knows his mission is coming to a climax: "We want to see Jesus" (12: 20–22). Indeed, as his enemies were only too well aware, "The whole world had gone after him" (12: 19). In John's Gospel Jesus is not abandoned on the cross, but draws disciples to Calvary with him. Joseph of Arimathea, a secret, fearful disciple, becomes bold at Jesus' burial (19: 38). Jesus' first resurrection appearance to Mary of Magdala in the garden draws her surprised affection. He immediately sends her to tell the good news (20: 17). All the disciples are sent to bear fruit (15: 8), to receive the Spirit, and to forgive sin (20: 21). And so, first drawn to Christ, we too are then sent by Christ.

As the Father sent Jesus, so Jesus missions his community of disciples. They are to continue his work, and do even greater things (14: 12). However, perhaps most important to John with his sacramental spirituality, the disciples and we along with them, are to be a sign: a sign that will attract the scattered, the lost and the lonely to a community of love and unity, a community who lives in Jesus as branches on a vine. "By this will all people know you are my disciples, if you love one another" (13: 35).

Jesus is *the* sacrament of God, and all of creation can be considered a sacrament of Christ. While bread, water, light, shepherds, vines and so much else point beyond, to Christ who is himself life in abundance, the sacrament of Jesus *par excellence* is the community of disciples: ourselves, the Church. After much reflection on their experience as Church, John's community questioned: How can we say we love God whom we cannot see if we are not loving the Church, our brothers and sisters whom we can see? (1 John 4: 20–21). We are sent as Jesus was sent. We who are closest to Jesus' heart are to make him known to the world.

Guided Prayer Passages

1 Corinthians 6: 12–20

> All things are lawful for me, but I will not be made a slave by anyone or anything. Food is for the stomach and the stomach is for food, but God will do away with both. The body is not meant for fornication but for the Lord, and the Lord is for the body. God raised the Lord and through his power will raise us up as well.
>
> Do you not know that your bodies are members of Christ? ... Do you not know that your body is a shrine of the Holy Spirit, which you have from God? You do not belong to yourself. You were bought for a price. So then, glorify God in your body.

Our bodies are gifts, bought at a great price. Paul speaks about food and sex here. What other aspects of your body concern you? Show your body, part by part, to God, who knows your every cell. Ask Jesus to lay his hands on your head, then to grasp your shoulders. How does it feel to be touched by him? Tell him, and if this frightens or angers you, stop. Jesus wants only your good.

If this is a good experience, then feel, in your imagination, Jesus claiming each part of your body. Invite him to be Lord of your body as a whole and in every part. Give him your fears about your body, past sins against your body (including neglect), your bodily weaknesses and limits. Give him your bodily strengths, your joy in your body. Give him your whole self.

Romans 12: 1–2

> I beg you, brothers and sisters, through the compassion of God, to present your bodies as a sacrifice to God, a living, holy, well-pleasing, and reasonable worship. Do not be conformed to this age but be transformed, renewing your mind,

so that you may prove what is the good, well-pleasing and perfect will of God.

Paul exhorts us to present our bodies "through the compassion of God." Can you believe that God "suffers-with," and "feels-with" you? What feelings arise within you in response? God becomes flesh, incarnate, in Jesus so that God can share all the weakness, insecurity, pain, weariness of our bodies. God desires the whole of us, our embodied selves. What response can you make now to God's desire? What response do you hope to make? Talk with God about your hopes and fears.

John 11: 51–52

Jesus died to gather into one family all the scattered children of God.

Ask the Spirit to remind you of all the relationships in your family, neighborhood, parish, city, country and in the family of nations where people are separated, scattered, raging with hatred for one another. How does this make you feel? What do you want? What does God passionately desire?

Jesus wanted our reconciliation and unity so desperately that not only did he demonstrate this overwhelming desire in his life but he "died to gather us all, the scattered children of God." He lay down his life so that we might be gathered together from afar. "And I, if I be lifted up, will draw all to myself." Picture him lifted up on the cross and image all colors and cultures and kinds of people approaching him, drawn by such great love that they forget their fears and differences and even hatreds as they come to him.

Pray with this verse a second time. In what ways are you personally scattered? Pulled apart? Not whole? Not integrated? Ask Jesus to gather you interiorly and to center you.

Where in your family, community, world interests do you need the power of Jesus' death and exaltation to gather people together? Pray for these situations. Then ask Jesus why gathering his people was so important to him. Keep a mental image of Jesus on the cross with the peoples of all nations and times — and yourself — coming to him. Ask him how he feels; respond to his feelings. You are sent to draw people to Jesus, to show how attractive he is. How is Jesus attractive to you? Tell him why you admire and love him.

1 John 3: 16–18

> If anyone has the goods of this world and sees his or her brother or sister in need, yet closes his or her heart, how does God's love dwell in such a one? Little children, let us not love in word or speech but let us love in work and in truth.

The above is both a word of comfort and a word of challenge. Reflect on your "laying down" even a bit of your life, your time, your attention, your energy. For whom have you laid down part of yourself? Why? What did your service mean for those who were (or are still being) served? What did it mean for you personally? How has your little bit of service impacted the whole Church? Ask the Spirit to help you respond to that last question.

Faith-sharing

When your small group gathers for faith-sharing, use the above scripture passages which you have prayed over as the basis for your sharing. Refer to the suggestions in the Invitation if needed.

Small Group Exercises

1. The New Testament offers various images of Church: John's vine, new family, community of disciples; Paul's Body of Christ. What other New Testament images come to mind? (Check 1 Peter 2: 9 for a few.) What are some images that speak to you personally? What images can your group brainstorm?
2. We, the Church, are called to be an attractive sign of Christ. We are called to be a sign of God's life and love in abundance, which is embodied today in our community of disciples. How has the Spirit begun to make that happen in your family, in this scripture-sharing group, in your parish, community, diocese, world? Share a specific story.

Concluding Prayer

Anointing is a sign of consecration. (The Greek word for "anointed" is *christos.*) Thus, Jesus is the Anointed One, the Christ. We were anointed in baptism and confirmation. In memory of that Christ-ening, anoint one another in your group. Use sweet-smelling oil, or add a drop of perfume to common oil. Sign the cross on the forehead of the person next to you, as you proclaim: "Your body is for the Lord ... glorify God in your body" (1 Cor 6: 13, 20). Then imagine all the anointed ones of God around the earth, as well as those who have gone before us in faith.

Together with this whole community pray Psalm 100:

> Praise the Lord, all peoples of the earth.
> Worship the Lord in gladness.
> Enter God's courts with songs of exulting.
> Know that the Lord is God; God made us.
> We are God's very own, a people God has fashioned. Alleluia!

10

Ourselves as Church: Sacrament of Love and Union

Spirit and Sacrament, two particular ways God graces and transforms us, also facilitate our response to God's initiative of loving us first in Jesus. In this chapter, we will first contemplate the Church as the community of love and union through the experience of John's community. Then we will examine Paul's teaching on love and union, including both married love and sexual union as sacraments of God's loving us. This prayerful study of Spirit and sacrament also touches on an amazing reality: Paul considers women as embodiments of the Spirit and co-workers with the Spirit. He views their bodies as sacraments, as a means of God's grace in the family.

Questions

- What images of Church, in union with Christ and with one another, can you let float to the surface of your mind? Ask the Spirit for help. Body of Christ, vine with fruitful branches, the flock tended by the Good Shepherd, the garden of God are some biblical images. What others?
- What non-biblical images surface? One nine year-old said the Church is like a jello salad: the Holy Spirit is the red jello, and all of us are the nuts and fruits, different shapes and colors and tastes. What images come to you?
- A hymn from the 1960s proclaimed: "The more I love you, the more I know I'm in love with my God." Who specifically in your life is a sacrament of your love and union with God?

❧ Who are your companions, the ones with whom you break bread? (In Latin, *panis* is bread and *com* is with.) Who are your friends, a circle closer to your heart? Who are your intimates, the ones who know you thoroughly and love you almost as unconditionally as God?

Scriptural Message

John

Union of Friends

According to the Fourth Gospel, the Paraclete and the Church are the fruit of Jesus' body given and his blood poured out. Our love and union with each other as Church is a sign, a sacrament of God's love and union with Jesus. The Paraclete is the active presence of the risen Lord among us.

Jesus and the Father know and love each other. Our love and union as Church is also to be a mutual knowing and loving. Not only is the mutual knowing and loving of God and Jesus a model for us, but it is the very source of our love and union with one another. It is the Spirit.

We remember that Jesus prayed the night before he died, expressing his deepest desire. Risen, he continues to pray for us:

> That they may be one, Father, I pray. I pray for those whom you have given me, for they belong to you. All mine are yours, and yours are mine. May they be one *as* you, Father, are in me and I am in you, may they be in us ... that they may be one *as* we are one, I in them and you in me, that they may become perfectly one, that the world may know ... that you have loved them *just as* you have loved me. (From Jn 17)

So much of the Fourth Gospel is about love, union, friendship and intimacy. Our union with each other is meant to mirror, to embody God's and Jesus' mutual love and indwelling. In this gospel, instead of loving our enemies, we are instructed to know and love our friends, but to know and love them as Jesus knows and loves us and as the Father knows and loves Jesus.

We human beings have deep needs for belonging, for being known, and for being accepted as we really are. In response to our thirsts, we often attempt to fill our needs in ways that are less than human, less than free. Who of us feels loved enough, appreciated enough? Who can rest in enough union? "Our hearts are restless," writes St. Augustine, "until they rest in Thee."

In response to our restlessness, Jesus promises to fill our hungers and thirsts with his own self, as we see in John. The Twelve acknowledge that Jesus satisfies their hungers for belonging: "To whom shall we go? You have the words of eternal life" (Jn 6: 68). And again, Jesus fills the Samaritan woman's thirst for respect, acceptance and love.

In John's Gospel, Jesus continually invites us to come to him. He has many ways of satisfying our needs, myriad ways to unite us with himself and through himself with each other. Jesus loves us as sinners, because we are sinners. Surely the Samaritan woman's story shines with this message. In John, Jesus loves his friends dearly, faults and all, and doesn't hesitate to speak of his love in the most intimate terms.

Jesus speaks of knowing us as the Father knows him and as he knows the Father. Knowing, in Hebrew understanding, means a union epitomized in sexual intercourse. The urge to lose ourselves in a loved one (as through sexual union) is meant to be fulfilled in Jesus' offer of union. "Lose yourself in me and you will find yourself," is the way songwriter Carey Landry paraphrases John 12: 25. It takes courage to lose ourselves in Christ. In losing ourselves, "falling into the earth and dying," we have to trust that we do not remain alone, but bring forth much fruit (12: 25). This surrender of our very self to Christ leads to freedom, the truth that sets free.

Making such a surrender is to risk vulnerability. No wonder Peter didn't want his feet washed (Jn 13: 8). Who feels free to be so naked, so vulnerable? It is probably just as difficult for us to let the Lord touch our feet as it was for Peter. Yet, in the foot-washing, Jesus institutes a sacrament of God's service.

After inspiring us to wash one another's feet, Jesus announces that he has changed his relationship with us. In various types of service, there is usually some inequality in the relationship. Here, Jesus challenges us to mutuality, the same mutuality found in the way he loves the Father and the Father loves him. So he proclaims, "No longer do I call you *servants*. I have called you *friends,* for all that I have heard from my Father I have made known to you" (15: 15). He invites us to know him at the deepest core of his being. Jesus shares his inner life, his spiritual life, his union with God. Jesus, in this verse, offers the best rationale for our faith-sharing!

Paul

The Ways of Union

Paul as well as John sees how love and union, not structure and order, are primarily what make us Church. Thus, besides the charisms for ministry, Paul highlights the gift of our bodies, the arena in which both human and divine love and union are experienced. According to Paul, our bodies are sources of grace for each other. Grace may be expressed in marriage, through the gift of sexuality, and may also be expressed through the gift of celibacy. Perhaps in no other area of Christian living has Paul been so misinterpreted as in the area of sexuality and marriage. By extension, he is also misunderstood in his supposed teaching about and treatment of women.

Paul understands sexual union and marriage in the context of the Body of Christ. By focusing on the gift of the human body, therefore, we recognize both celibacy and marriage as equal gifts given to members of the Body. What does Paul actually say in this regard?

In 1 Corinthians, chapter seven, Paul reflects on these two different choices as gifts of God for the building up of the body that is the Church. According to the Second Vatican Council, marriage and celibacy are two vocations, two different ways of discipleship. All other ministry, be it politics or priesthood, medicine or mothering, praying for or playing with the disadvantaged, is done from our basic commitment in love and union, expressed either in marriage or in celibacy.

Paul responds to questions raised by his young community located in Corinth, the "sin city" of the ancient world. Orgies and promiscuity were rampant. Many of the new Christians had just recently left that lifestyle. As a reaction to their former ways, some of the new converts went to the other extreme and decided to abstain from sex even in marriage. Thus, Paul opens the seventh chapter of his first letter to Corinth with, "You say it is good for a man to have nothing to do with women...." Here, he is quoting the Corinthians' misguided thinking, which is how this must be understood.

Paul continues: "The husband must give the wife her due" (7: 3), a startling statement in favor of women. In ancient Jewish society a woman had nothing due her, absolutely no rights; in Greek society she was scarcely more honored. Being "in Christ," however, radically changes the relationship in marriage and makes the partners equal: "In Christ there is no ... male or female for you are all one in Christ Jesus" (Gal 3: 28). Even more startling is Paul's teaching on mutuality in marriage: "The husband cannot claim his body as his own; it is his wife's" (1 Cor 7: 4).

"To the unmarried men and to the widows, I say, it is good to stay as I am" (1 Cor 7: 8), usually has been interpreted as Paul being himself celibate, or at least widowed. As a rabbi, Paul would have had to be married; his wife may have died or may share his mission: "Haven't I the right to take a *gyne* (woman or wife; it means both) with me as does Peter?" (1 Cor 9:5; NRSV has a footnote: "a sister as a wife"). "Stay as I am" (7: 8) may mean devoted totally to evangelization, as Paul was. Whatever helps to focus the desires of the married, the unmarried and the widowed on the work of the Lord is the "gift God has granted" (7: 7), whether granted in marriage or celibacy.

At a time when the major Jewish rabbis permitted a man to divorce his wife for putting too much salt in his food, Jesus' saying against divorce (Mk 10: 2–12) must have offered Jewish-Christian women refuge from arbitrary divorce practices. Paul implies that in her new freedom "in Christ," a Christian woman, as an equal to her husband, could divorce her husband but she should not (1 Cor 7: 10–11).

The First Letter to the Corinthians (7: 14–16) offers one of the most beautiful expressions of what a Christian family is. A Christian spouse is a channel of grace for the non-Christian spouse. A woman's body, a man's body, their sexual union, their daily living in love, are sources of grace, of union with God. Their love, in all its aspects, is sacrament. Because of the Christian in a family, "your children belong to God," a very important teaching in a time when there was no infant baptism.

The same chapter in 1 Corinthians, which lauds marriage and sex as a channel of grace in the family, includes a puzzling passivity in Paul. He does not denounce slavery (7: 17–24) as one would expect. It seems that Paul takes for granted that this injustice is about to end. This can provide a context for what follows on the topic of celibacy. Paul was utterly certain that, with the resurrection of Jesus, the end time had begun. Everything, including slavery and marriage, was passing away. God was gathering the nations together as Isaiah had promised, and the time was short before the return of the risen Lord in glory.

Paul had eagerly joined God's work as an ambassador of reconciliation (2 Cor 5: 19–20), especially oriented to the Gentiles. He was urgent in his preaching the good news, and he hoped to enlist as many of the newly baptized in his urgent mission. "This world as we know it is passing away" (7: 31). How to concentrate the energy of the new Christians in such apocalyptic times? Paul offers a way to focus in chapter seven, verses 32–34:

> I want you to be without anxieties. The unmarried man cares about the things of the Lord, how he may please the Lord, but the married man cares about worldly responsibilities, and how he may please his wife. He is divided.
>
> The unmarried woman and the virgin care for the things of the Lord. Thus she may become holy in body and in spirit. But the married woman cares about her responsibilities and how she may please her husband.

Paul and Women

If love and union are at the core of our community, then all forms of division must be healed "in Christ." And while racism, classism, nationalism, misuse of hierarchical status, and religious wars affect certain people and cultures, every human being is affected by sexism. Some even mistakenly attribute sexism to Paul without verifying the authorship of certain writings.

For example, 1 Timothy was not written by Paul, but by later disciples. In 2:15, the author exhorts women: "By your child bearing you will save your souls." But, however exalted the Christian family may be for Paul, we have already seen that neither motherhood nor fatherhood, nor anything at all saves us except the dying and resurrection of Jesus. Paul's central teaching is that *no work of ours but only God saves us* through Jesus Christ. Also, as a Jew, Paul would not have split the human person into body/soul. In Paul's mental categories, God does not save "souls" but the whole person. Nor do we "save our own souls" for that matter. Salvation is God's work. And finally, as recorded in 1 Corinthians 7, Paul prefers that women who may receive the gift of celibacy not marry and bear children, but rather remain celibate in order to devote themselves to mission and ministry.

Marriage and sex are truly gifts and sacraments of salvation, as Paul has already established. But because of his belief in "these urgent times," his hope echoes Jesus' own saying that celibacy is a gift for the sake of God's reign, not because it has any value in itself (Mt 19: 12). We can easily imagine male celibates engaged in preaching, teaching and exhorting for the sake of the God's reign: "Be reconciled, for the time is short." What is remarkable is that Paul urged women to do the same. Women "co-labored" with Paul, some probably at his express invitation, some probably celibate women like Phoebe of Cenchreae, an officer "on mission" to Rome (Rom 16: 1–2).

Ancient manuscripts contain obscure verses in 1 Corinthians 7: 36–38. The New English Bible translates it best: "If a man has a partner in celibacy ..." It seems that Christian men and women may have teamed in their mission work, even sharing a home in a society unfriendly to women's independence. A woman celibate could probably not live on her own without scandal in the ancient Greco-Roman society. Paul may be encouraging a non-genital man/woman relationship in which both partners would be devoted to the Christian mission. If their love becomes genitally oriented, Paul writes: "There is nothing wrong in it; let them marry.... Thus, he who marries his partner does well, and he who does not will do better."

If that last clause seems to destroy the argument about separate but equal gifts of marriage and celibacy, it is only because, to Paul's mind, everything is passing away. Paul is not against sex, marriage or women. He simply urges the Corinthians in apocalyptic times to devote their entire selves to the mission. That particular kind of freedom and availability for mission is usually easier for the unmarried.

In reinterpreting Paul on marriage, we need not downplay the gift of celibacy. Celibacy, not as requirement but as gift, surely will always be given to certain members of the Body for the sake of God's reign. For the sake of mission, this gift will flourish.

Celibacy can, and hopefully does, lead to human intimacy and permanent commitment. Marriage can, and hopefully does, lead to freedom for ministry. Neither way is higher or more perfect. Both are for the building up of the Body.

Gifts of Love and Compassion

The married and the celibate both express themselves through loving. At the end of his list of charisms in Romans, Paul pens a hymn to love in which he marshals action words to depict love: "Let love be genuine: shrinking from evil, clinging to good, loving warmly, preferring one another, in zeal not slothful, burning in spirit, serving the Lord, rejoicing in hope, enduring in affliction, steadfastly continuing in prayer, sharing the needs of the saints, practicing hospitality" (Rom 12: 9–15). The hymn continues to elaborate on sharing with the saints, who for Paul were all Christians, living and dead. He writes, "Rejoice with those rejoicing, weep with those weeping" (Rom 12: 15).

For Paul, a kind of ultimate consequence of being together in Christ is compassion: rejoicing with, weeping with, suffering with (1 Cor 12: 26), being with, thinking with (Rom 12: 16), feeling with one another. He writes the Galatian community, "Be as I am, because I am as you are" (Gal 4: 12), and describes his empathy, "Who is weak and I am not weak?" (2 Cor 11: 29).

Paul can lead us along this way, however, because he has first experienced God as the Father of compassion and the God of all comfort (2 Cor 1: 3; Rom 12: 1). If God pours God's own self into our hearts (Rom 5: 5), then Paul understands the gospel command of love not as law but as sharing, participating in God's own compassion. If we must have the law, then Paul proclaims it to be the law of compassion: "Bear one another's burdens, and so you will make full the law of Christ" (Gal 6: 2).

In Romans 13: 8–10, in the context of justice in the public sphere, Paul does use a kind of legal language: "Owe no one anything except to love one another." He explains how all the commandments are summed up in the law of love. Yet, Paul offers neither an ethical code nor a moral system. Love is a spiritual gift, a charism, one of the fruits of the Holy Spirit, a share in God's own love made available and tangible in Christ Jesus. The bond of the Body, the life-blood of the Body, the Spirit of whom we all drink, the greatest of all gifts, is love.

The reality is that, in all our weakness and sin, we are already surrendered in love to the risen Lord. Paul expresses this union and the action that results as a "pressing forward to take hold of Christ who has already taken hold of me" (Phil 3: 12). Paul often writes that we are "in Christ Jesus." To be *in* Christ Jesus is not to live in a cosmic, ethereal atmosphere. It is to live, as the scripture scholar Barnabas Ahern, C.P., once said, "in an intimate bond of affection and dependence uniting two real persons." Being "in Christ" is like being "in love." Being in Christ is neither a statement of doctrine nor of belonging to the Church. It is a suffusion of our whole life, in love.

Guided Prayer Passages

Teresa of Avila calls prayer a conversation with Someone whom we know loves us, and an essential part of any conversation is listening. To listen to the Spirit, I suggest a prayer called the "bubble up" prayer, based on Jesus' promise of the Spirit in the Fourth Gospel, "rivers of living water deep within" (7: 38). Ask the Spirit to let "bubble up" from deep within you, for example, all God's gifts to you throughout your life. Ask the Spirit to convince you that you are special in the eyes of God and truly loved, that your gifts are unique, and that you are needed for the building up of the whole Church-community.

To experience the "bubble-up" prayer, ask the Spirit to let you hear the Spirit's prayer within you, to teach you. Ask the Spirit, and then sit quietly and see what "bubbles up" to your consciousness. Don't try to think and introspect. Let the realization of how you are loved and gifted "come" to you as you try to listen to the Spirit's response. What is God's purpose in gifting you? Ask the Spirit. Then listen and let the response simply "bubble up." Later you may want to record what you learn.

1 John 4: 18–20

> Fear has no place in love. Perfect love casts out fear.... We love because we are first loved. If anyone says, "I love God," and hates his brother or sister in Christ, that person is a liar. For the one who does not love the brother or sister who can be seen cannot love God who is not seen.

We opened this last set of prayers by asking the Spirit to let "bubble up" from deep within all the ways in which God has gifted us. Surely, one of God's purposes in gifting us is to help us relax, knowing and trusting how well-loved we are. And yet many of us are afraid: afraid of God, afraid we're not good enough for God, afraid of brothers and sisters who think and believe differently from us. Fear can lead to hatred, and John's community asks: How can we say we love God whom we don't see, when we hate the brother or sister whom we do see?

Pray passionately that divisions in the Body be healed, that factions and sects be reconciled. Beg God to soothe fearful hearts and to soften hearts hardened in judgment against other members of Christ's own Body. Pray that God's perfect love casts out fear and heals any trace of fear or judgment that lingers within your own heart.

1 Corinthians 12: 4–13

> There are a variety of gifts, but the same Spirit who gives them; there are many ways to serve, but one Lord is served; there are many kinds of work, but it is the same God who gives ability to each. The presence of the Spirit is shown

in each of us for the good of all. The Spirit gives one person a message full of wisdom, while to another the Spirit gives a word of knowledge. The one Spirit gives faith to one, the power to heal to another, the ability to do mighty works to yet another. One receives the gift of proclaiming God's message, another the ability to discern which gifts are of the Spirit and which are not. The Spirit leads one to speak in tongues, and another to interpret these foreign words. It is one and the same Spirit who does all this, giving a unique gift to each person.

Christ is a single body. It has many different parts, yet it is one body. So all of us, whether Jews or Gentiles, whether slaves or free, have been baptized, plunged into one body by the one Spirit. We have all been given the same Spirit to drink.

Ask the Spirit to reveal what gifts you have that are given to you for the building up of the Body (your family, your community, your country). Your gifts may not necessarily be those from Paul's list, and certainly not limited to these.

Then ask the Spirit to remind you of someone you know who has a particular gift mentioned by Paul. How do you feel about that person? Tell the Spirit your feelings. Proud? Jealous? Keep asking the Spirit (every day) to show you your own gifts.

Philippians 2: 7

If there is any comfort *(parakaleo)* in Christ, if any consolation in love, any community of spirit, any compassion and sympathy, then make my joy complete by thinking together, loving well, one spirit, one heart. Do nothing in a spirit of rivalry or taking the glory, but in humility, consider the other as surpassing. Do not get so caught up in your own concerns that you do not pay attention to the cares of others.

Have this mind in you as in Christ Jesus who, although in the form of God, did not think equality with God something to be clung to. He emptied himself, taking the form of a slave, becoming as all human beings are.

This is another Pauline hymn of love that makes compassion central. A literal translation of the first line reads, " ... any community *(koinonia)* of spirit, and gut-level compassion."

Ask to know the comfort of Christ. Then wait silently, open to receive. With whom do you have "community of spirit"? With whom do you want it? Family? Coworkers? Neighbors? The homeless and hungry? Folks of another race? Another nation? Another religion? Christians who do not believe as you do? With whom does God want you to have "community of spirit"? Share all your fears and desires with Christ, present in you and in them.

Philippians 2: 5

Have this mind in you which was also in Christ Jesus.

Jesus was of a mind to empty himself, even to experience "separation" from God in the simple fact of being human. He did not cling to being God, and yet, he was in God. To what do you cling? Instead of scraping your conscience, ask Jesus to show you. Of what do you want to be emptied? How does Jesus feel about that? Try to listen to him. Ask Jesus to bring you into the lifelong process of not only being emptied but of being filled, of being and ever more becoming "in Christ." Ask Jesus to cling to you while you try to cling to him.

2 Corinthians 1: 3-5

Blessed be the God and Father of our Lord Jesus Christ, the father of mercies and the God of all consolation. God comforts us in our afflictions. Thus we are able to console those who have many troubles with the same comfort which we have received from God. Just as we have a share in Christ's many sufferings, so through Christ we share in God's great consolation.

Ask Jesus to help you remember some difficult situations in the past month.

How did your living through those difficulties lead you in any way to grow in compassion for others? Ask to have the heart of Christ so you may comfort others in their sufferings. Pray for some of those who are suffering now.

Galatians 6:2

Bear one another's burden and so you will fulfill the law of Christ.

Ask for the fullness of the Spirit who is love and who is burden-bearer. The Spirit is your power and energy to love. Share some of your burdens in loving with the Spirit.

1 John 4: 18

Perfect love casts out fear.

God embodied in Jesus is the only one capable of perfect love. What are your fears involved in belonging, in knowing someone deeply, in risking to share your ideas, decisions, feelings, dreams, successes and failures with another, in laying down your life for your friends? What are your specific fears of intimacy?

John 15: 9–17

"As the Father has loved me, I also have loved you…. I have spoken these things to you so that I may have joy in you and that your joy may be complete…. I have called you friends."

Jesus deeply and passionately desires that you be in union with him. Remember moments or events when you felt united with him and/or others. "... So that I may have joy in you and your joy may be complete." Can you hear Jesus speak directly to you, telling you that you are the cause of his emotion, the cause of his joy? How do you feel? Speak with him about these feelings.

You are the one whom Jesus calls "friend." His whole life expresses his consuming desire to be with you. How do you feel about his desire to share your life? Tell Jesus what it means to you to have him be so intimately present to you. What do you want to share with him?

1 Corinthians 13: 13

... and the greatest of these is love.

Love is the greatest gift that God gives us. It is a gift, not our achievement. Love is God's own self, poured into our hearts, lavished on us, in so many ways, through so many people. What is your experience of being loved? Recall your earliest memory ... your dearest friend ... various friends/children loving you in different ways. Recall the greatest sacrifice made for your sake ... the most quiet, most shy action of love offered you ... your most recent experience of being loved.

What is your experience of loving? Your earliest memory? (Use again the above questions.) Hopefully, you are in a quiet, grateful, peaceful state. "Rest a while."

Faith-sharing

When your small group gathers for faith-sharing, use the above scripture passages which you have prayed over as the basis for your sharing. Refer to the suggestions in the Invitation if needed.

Small Group Exercises

These exercises may take more than one, even more than two sessions.

1. After pondering the gifts listed in Paul's hymn to love (Rom 12: 9–13), mention the names of people your group might know (public or parish figures or members of the group) who love:

   - by shrinking from evil and clinging to good;
   - warmly;
   - preferring the other to self;
   - zealously, burning in spirit;
   - genuinely;
   - serving the Lord;
   - rejoicing in hope;
   - enduring in affliction;
   - steadfastly continuing in prayer;
   - sharing the needs of the saints;
   - practicing hospitality.

   Conclude with a prayer of thanksgiving that the Spirit has poured so much love into human hearts.

2. To become more aware of our bodies can be a prelude to contemplation. Spend ten minutes of silence in your group sensing your own face, although you can't see or hear it. What is happening on, in, to your chin? Your cheek? Your eyelid, and so on. Then discuss your experience.

   Now spend ten minutes concentrated on your own breathing. After five minutes of paying attention to your breathing, let a leader guide the group. Slowly, with pauses between, let the leader suggest out loud to the group:

Breathe God in ...
Breathe in God's truth ...
Breathe in God's beauty ...
Breathe in God's love ...
Breathe God in deeply ...
Breathe out whatever angers you ...
Breathe out your pride ...
Breathe out your worries ...
Breathe out your little greeds ...
Breathe deeply and breathe in God ...
Breathe in the peace of God ...
Breathe in God's joy ...
Breathe in the love who is God ...

After a few minutes of silence, share with the group, not the content of your angers or worries, but your feelings throughout the exercise.

3. In our study of John's final chapters, we entered the story of Jesus' Last Supper, passion, death, resurrection and his risen appearances. What has your own experience of John's Gospel been throughout this prayerful study? What are your feelings about the unique way John portrays Jesus' living, teaching, dying and rising?

Through our study of Paul, how has your relationship with Paul changed in the course of this prayer/study? Share your insights and/or your feelings with your group.

4. By now, as you conclude this book, your group should know each other quite well. This exercise asks you to celebrate the gifts of one another. You might like to set it in the context of a prayer service.

Take a sheet of paper for each member of the group. In silence, look at a group member and bring to mind his or her gifts shared in this group, or gifts you have observed in other situations. Write the member's name and then list these gifts. Begin a new sheet for the second person, etc. Collect all papers for Bill in one pile, Jean in another, etc. ...

Then give the papers listing Bill's gifts to someone else in the group, perhaps to Jean, to read. Give Jean's gifts to Joe, etc. ... Let the lists of gifts be read slowly, reverently, so that group members are proclaiming each other's gifts aloud. At the end of the proclamation, give each member his or her own lists of gifts.

Concluding Prayer

Leader:

The Word was made flesh and pitched a tent, living among us.

Reader:

A reading from the prophet Isaiah:

Listen to my word and you will have food to eat. Come and listen to my words. Hear me and you shall have life. The word which comes from my mouth shall not return to me fruitless. My word will accomplish my purpose. And you, you will go forward in joy. You will be led forth in peace. (From Isaiah 55)

Three members may pray the following response from Psalm 119:

Reader One:

Enable me to speak the true message at all times; let me sing of your love and your wisdom.

Reader Two:
> Give me your wisdom and your knowledge, because I trust in your word.

Reader Three:
> With open mouth I pant with desire for your word. Fill me, Lord, with your truth.

Together:
> Lord Jesus, we praise and thank you for all the love you have lavished on this, our little community of disciples. Send us the fullness of your Spirit so that we may continue to embody your life and love wherever you send us from this group. Let your light shine in our hearts and in our actions that we may be your sacrament in the world. Let your fountains well up in us and your bread nourish not only ourselves but our world. Let your Paraclete teach us truth and set us free. Live in us more completely, Lord Jesus, so that all people may see the sign of your life and may glorify our God. We ask this in your name and in the power of your Spirit.
>
> Let everyone extend both hands over the group, praying silently in blessing. Conclude with a kiss of peace.

Conclusion

During the time spent with this book, all our prayer and group work has simply been a spelling out of what our being, knowing, loving and doing "in Christ" is all about. In a sense, this book is a reflection on the meaning of our baptism into Christ Jesus, where Spirit and sacrament are first publicly expressed in our lives, and our being transformed from glory to glory begins.

We have pondered:

- How finding God in all things is celebrating the sacramentality of life;
- How the dying and resurrection of Jesus is the event in which both Paul and John locate God's love poured out in history;
- How God's love is poured out in Christ while we were not only sinners, but even God's enemies;
- How the Spirit of Jesus, yet another expression of God's love, is poured out in Christ;
- How being in Christ means being the Body of Christ, the visible sign, the very sacrament of God's love bestowed;
- How we are gifted with love and compassion for all others, those who know that they are in Christ and those to whom we, the Church, will offer this good news.

Wherever we go, lured by and sent by the Spirit to *be* the sacrament of Christ, we journey "in Christ," who has taken hold of us as really as he took hold of Paul, as really as he captured the hearts and minds of John's community. Jesus is God's lavished love, the ultimate gift of God's own self. That love of God — that unconditional, abundant, extravagant, faithful, steady, everlasting compassion of God — is made available to us "in Christ," and through us, in the Spirit, to the world.

Having completed this book, perhaps each group member could now gather and lead a new group on this journey with Paul and John. You will be amazed, as you study and pray with the same passages again, how much more deeply the Word of God will touch and transform you.

Or, if your group prefers to stay together, try contemplatively working through John's entire gospel, or one of Paul's letters. (First Corinthians, with its focus on community, would make a good beginning.)

Know that I will be praying for you all, throughout my life and after this life as well, thanking God for our relationship in Christ Jesus and his Spirit.

Bibliography

Bonhoeffer, Dietrich. *Life Together.* New York: Harper & Row, 1954.
Brown, Raymond, S.S. *The Community of the Beloved Disciple.* Mahwah, NJ: Paulist Press, 1979.
____.*The Gospel According to John.* Anchor Bible. 2 vols. Garden City, NY: Doubleday, 1966.
Campbell, Joan. *Kinship Relations in the Gospel of John.* Washington, DC: The Catholic Biblical Association of America, 2007.
Cardenal, Ernesto. *The Gospel in Solentiname.* 4 vols. Maryknoll, NY: Orbis Books, 1976.
Cooke, Bernard. *Sacraments and Sacramentality.* Mystic, CT: Twenty-Third Publications, 1983.
Dodd, C.H. *The Interpretation of the Fourth Gospel.* Cambridge, England: University Press, 1968.
Donovan, Vincent. *Christianity Rediscovered.* Maryknoll, NY: Orbis Books, 1978.
Dougherty, Rose Mary, SSND. *Discernment.* Mahwah, NJ: Paulist Press, 2009.
Duffy, Regis, O.F.M. *On Becoming a Catholic.* San Francisco: Harper & Row, 1984.
____. *Real Presence.* San Francisco: Harper & Row, 1982.
Gardner, WH and MacKenzie, NH. *The Poems of Gerard Manley Hopkins.* 4th ed. London: Oxford University Press, 1970.
Gorman, Michael. *Reading Paul.* Eugene, OR: Cascade Books, 2008
Gutierrez, Gustavo. *A Theology of Liberation.* Maryknoll, NY: Orbis Books, 1973.
Harrington, Daniel, SJ. *Meeting St. Paul Today.* Chicago: Loyola Press, 2009.
Hellwig, Monica. *Eucharist and the Hungers of the World.* New York: Paulist Press, 1977.
Hengel, Martin. *The Pre-Christian Paul.* London: SCM Press, 1991.
Levine, Amy-Jill, ed. *A Feminist Companion to Paul.* London: T&T Clark International, 2004.
McDermott, Brian, S.J. *What Are They Saying About The Grace of Christ?* Mahwah, NJ: Paulist Press, 1984.
____.*Word Become Flesh.* New Theology Studies. Collegeville: Glazier/Liturgical, 1993.
McDonnell, Rea, SSND. *When God Comes Close.* Boston: Pauline Books and Media, 1994.

———. *Why, God? A Glimpse into the Mystery of Suffering.* Hyde Park, NY: New City Press, 2002.

Monden, Louis. *Sin, Liberty, and Law.* New York: Sheed and Ward, 1965.

Murphy-O'Connor, Jerome, O.P. *Becoming Human Together: The Pastoral Anthropology of St. Paul.* Collegeville, MN: Michael Glazier, 1982.

Neyrey, Jerome, SJ. *The Gospel of John.* Cambridge: Cambridge University Press, 2007.

O'Day, Gail and Susan Hylen. *John.* Louisville, KY: Westminster John Knox Press, 2006.

Perkins, Pheme. *Ministering in the Pauline Churches.* Mahwah, NJ: Paulist Press, 1982.

Rahner, Karl, S.J. *The Love of Jesus and the Love of Neighbor.* New York: Crossroad, 1981.

Reicke, Bo. *Re-Examining Paul's Letters.* Harrisburg, PA: Trinity Press International, 2001.

Robinson, Bishop John A. T. *The Body.* London: SCM Press Ltd., 1952.

Samra, James. *Being Conformed to Christ in Community.* London: T&T Clark, 2006.

Shea, John. *An Experience Named Spirit.* Chicago: The Thomas More Press, 1983.

Tobin, Thomas, SJ. *The Spirituality of Paul.* Collegeville, MN: Michael Glazier, 1987.

www.ingramcontent.com/pod-product-compliance
Lightning Source LLC
Chambersburg PA
CBHW071712090426
42738CB00009B/1744